The Signature of the World

Also available from Continuum:

The Signature of the World,

Or,

What is Deleuze and Guattari's Philosophy?

ÉRIC ALLIEZ

Translated by
ELIOT ROSS ALBERT
and
ALBERTO TOSCANO

Preface by
ALBERTO TOSCANO

continuum
NEW YORK • LONDON

CONTINUUM

The Tower Building
11 York Road
London SE1 7NX

15 East 26th Street
New York
NY 10010

English translation © Continuum 2004

Originally published as *La Signature du Monde* by Les Éditions du Cerf, Paris.

British Library Cataloguing-in-Publication Data
A catalogue record for this book is available from the British Library.

ISBN: HB: 0-8264-5620-0
PB: 0-8264-5621-9

Library of Congress Cataloging-in-Publication Data
A catalog record of this book is available from the Library of Congress.

Typeset by Servis Filmsetting Ltd, Manchester
Printed and bound in Great Britain by
MPG Books Ltd, Bodmin, Cornwall

Contents

Presentation

Despite the critiques aimed at them, each and every day ontologies are reborn under our gaze, if not from out of our own discourses. The need that pushes towards this rebirth is most often satisfied by the authority of established fact, with no effort being made to know the conditions behind this need and, by the same token, the limits of its validity. We thus witness the formation of all manner of hybrid systems, halfway between ideology and erudite bricolage, whose historical usefulness consists in exorcizing, each and every time, our great fear of modernity. By restoring, in the most varied guises, the absolute immanence of objective reality, such systems serve to unburden the modern subject of the weight of his autonomy, authorizing him to merge, according to Adorno's formula, into 'a heteronomous order exempted from the demand to justify itself before consciousness'.

We should therefore recall that there is no common measure between the more or less skilful, naïve tirades of the adepts of reified knowledge and the methodical speculations of an authentic thinker. Whatever our idea of philosophy may be, it is in our interest to welcome the most vigorous attempts to give satisfaction to the primordial needs of intelligence, beginning with the ontological need. Such attempts renew, well beyond the narrow and timid resubstantializations, which mark out the course of science, the original challenge of metaphysics.

There is no doubt that Éric Alliez's fine text is to be counted among the exemplary successes in this renewal of ontology. By restoring, with equal doses of rigour and talent, the joint intuitions of Gilles Deleuze and Félix Guattari – to whose memory this book is dedicated – he allows us to appreciate what ontology is still capable of today.

Heinz Wismann[1]

---

[1] [This is the back cover text written for *La signature du monde* by the editor of the 'Passages' series in which it first appeared for the Éditions du Cerf. All notes in brackets are the translators'.]

Preface: The Coloured Thickness of a Problem

A new Meno would say: it is knowledge that is nothing more than an empirical figure, a simple result which continually falls back into experience; whereas learning is the true transcendental structure which unites difference to difference, dissimilarity to dissimilarity, without mediating between them – not in the form of a mythical past or former present, but in the pure form of an empty time in general.
Gilles Deleuze, *Difference and Repetition*

The strictures of quality assessment and the self-reinforcing imperatives of the market have consigned philosophers, as of late, to a regime of publication – of *poubéllication*, to adopt Lacan's portmanteau quip – dominated by the exhaustive introduction, the definitive treatment or the comparative exercise in ecumenical interdisciplinarity. What is most insidious about this synoptic regime, whose hegemony is strongest in the Atlantic, or Anglo-American, sphere, is that its steady, irrepressible advance takes place under the seemingly unimpeachable banner of *pedagogy*. This predicament is all the more symptomatic when it comes to the presentation of thinkers gathered under the exquisitely equivocal heading of 'Continental'. In this instance, we are faced with a generalized practice of reduction of complexity ('the gnomic, impenetrable dicta of philosopher X finally made *clear, accessible* . . .') uneasily accompanied by the claim, often emblazoned on the book's packaging, that what we are dealing with is the 'most radical', 'newest', 'most extreme' intellectual project to date. It is rarely the case that the claims made on behalf of the thinker under consideration exert any influence on the approach, the style, the mode of presentation. A kind of degree-zero of writing, unaware of itself, often suffices. In the case of Deleuze and Guattari, this serves to exacerbate the paradox of an ideal of untrammelled communication being put to the service of a philosophy which condemns that very ideal as a capitulation to opinion (*doxa*), as a collusion with the most reductive and regressive tendencies in contemporary capitalism. This situation, the outcome of a disciplinary conjuncture which sees the circulation of ideas being ever more restricted to a wilfully pre-constituted 'projected readership' is all the more difficult to resist inasmuch as it is driven by a forced (re)production of the 'new', which, to all intents and purposes, makes the promotion of the unexpected into the sine qua non of intellectual life. But, as *What is Philosophy?* and *The Signature of the World* tell us, the concepts of philosophy are not the distant cousins of the ones constantly hatched in the polished interiors of advertising companies around the globe. Or, to take the point a bit further, everything points to the conclusion that a philosophy moulded by the demands of marketing is necessarily a philosophy incapable of thinking in and through capitalism.

The reasons why these questions of philosophical culture and transmission might be aggravated when the work of Deleuze and Guattari is at stake do not just boil down to these authors' engagement with the question of capitalism and their trenchant polemic against its regimes of communication and consumption. Both in collaboration and in their separate writings, Deleuze and Guattari foreground the issue of pedagogy and the related notion of apprenticeship, with remarkable insistence (it would not be otiose to contrast their efforts on this score with those of contemporaries such as Lacan, Derrida or Rancière or, perhaps more fruitfully, with the overt preoccupations of American pragmatism). The crux of the matter is that pedagogy is not restricted to a set of operations aimed at facilitating access to a pre-existing object, nor, conversely, is it a divining practice that coaxes, from a subject of teaching, some latent cognitive content. Following upon Spinoza's treatment of the common notions, Deleuze, in *Difference and Repetition*, subtracts apprenticeship, or *learning*, from the representational logic of instruction, making it into a matter of the sub-representational contemplation or, better, *contraction*, of singularities, into the ability to extract a material schematism, or spatio-temporal dynamism, out of one's encounter with what he elsewhere terms, following Blanchot, the outside of thought. In view of Alliez's distinctive concern with the sensible conditions of philosophy, science and art, with the transversal character of *aisthesis* as both affect and experiment, passive synthesis and invention, it is important to note the intimate bond between philosophical apprenticeship and the question of sensibility as presented by Deleuze. It is this bond, sealed by the dependence of conceptualization on an encounter, which turns learning away from an objective *method* and toward the necessarily 'subliminal' nature of the Idea, making philosophical *culture* into something other than (scientific) *knowledge*. As Deleuze writes: 'There is no more a method for learning than there is a method for finding treasures, but a violent training, a culture or *paideïa* which affects the entire individual [. . .]. Method is the means of that knowledge which regulates the collaboration of all the faculties. It is therefore the manifestation of a common sense or the realisation of a *Cogitatio natura*, and presupposes a good will as though this were a "premeditated decision" of the thinker. Culture, however, is an involuntary adventure, the movement of learning which links a sensibility, a memory and then a thought, with all the cruelties and violence necessary . . .' Learning, and the indirect apprenticeship that a commentary constitutes, are thus not vanishing mediators between an initial situation of non-knowledge or ignorance and a final state of completed – which is to say representable – knowledge. Instead, as the constitution or invention of a determinate or differentiated problematic field, learning is the very essence of philosophy as an experience of construction whose concern is not with the production of stable propositions in a present voided of virtuality or becoming. As a truly transcendental exercise, learning (and the commentary as one of the guises learning takes) eschews the empirical actuality of a solution, endeavouring instead to link the subjectivity of the apprentice (or the commentator) to 'the singular points of the objective in order to form a problematic field'. Rather than as a mediator between the (ignorant) reader and the (final) text or doctrine, a commentary can thus be conceived as a novel problematization of the ideal connections that define a particular philosophical object, a repetition of the text that does not seek to identify its theses as much as turn heterogeneity into consistency, uniting differences to differences, and open the work in question both to the 'empty time' or Aion of the event and to the specific virtualities of a contemporary situation.

Expanding upon some of the pedagogical suggestions offered by *Difference and Repetition*, *What is Philosophy?*, with its exploration of the auto-positional nature of the concept, provocatively enjoins us to think the *pedagogy* of the concept, the delineation of its parameters of construction and components, as being one with the pedagogy *of the concept*, the concept's own becoming and variability with regard to 'its' encounters with a non-philosophical outside. Likewise for the notion, delved into at length by Alliez both in the main text and the appendices, of a *phenomenology of the concept*, in which the cognitive, perceptual and sensory attributes of the concept are, in the order of construction, prior to any ascription of phenomenological properties to (the concept of) a subject. The tensions and contradictions raised by subjecting the work of Deleuze and Guattari to what I initially called the synoptic regime are compounded once we consider the correlate to the pedagogy of the concept, the *stratigraphic* revolution in the practice of the history of philosophy. Here lies perhaps the most significant contribution of Alliez's own work, which, beginning with *Capital Times*, combines (1) a radical recasting of the very notion of philosophical history, (2) a polemical genealogy of modernity understood in terms of different conduits of time, as these relate to the constitution of capitalism and (3) a reactivation through virtualization of past philosophies and their distinctive temporalities. Despite the somewhat heavy-handed dichotomy of geology and genealogy in *What is Philosophy?*, we can say that both a stratigraphic approach and a counter-genealogy of the kind practiced by Alliez are committed to treating philosophers and their concepts outside of the linearity, continuity and divisibility that characterize the customary teaching of the history of philosophy. By the same token, they view the reactivation of the virtualities of a given philosophy in terms of their potentially subversive reinsertion into a present conjuncture, which is why, as Alliez writes, 'from a philosophical point of view, the history of philosophy is only worth our while if it begins to introduce some philosophical time into the time of history', according to a 'principle of contingent reason' that remains attentive to the intimate resonances between the singularities of a concept and non-philosophical becomings and events. Whence an open battle against any brand of teleology in the history of philosophy, whether this be the moral teleology of Critique, the dialectical teleology of self-consciousness or the passive nihilism that characterizes the anti-teleological teleology of postmodernism, the litany of the end of philosophy. Against all these options and tendencies, Deleuze and Guattari, as Negri has noted, present us with 'a discontinuous history of singularity'.

Whilst today's pseudo-scholasticism is set on the saturation of secondary markets dominated by canonized names (even when the canon is a canon of 'marginals'), there is in the work of Alliez, as informed by his own ongoing and innovative research into the tensions and transformations in Mediaeval and Renaissance thought that set the stage for the divergent trajectories of philosophical modernity and its dialogue with the groundbreaking efforts of contemporary historians of philosophy such as Alain de Libera and Jean-François Courtine, a rare sensitivity to the sheer daring and intellectual complexity manifested by the scholastic practice of reading and commentary. What transpires from this attention to and reactivation of mediaeval textual practices is both a novel style of philosophical composition and a very distinctive approach to the history, or better genealogy, of philosophy, as well as the complex relationship between philosophical invention and philosophical historiography. Much like the writings of the mediaeval commentators, it is fair to say that *The Signature of the World* is not at all an 'easier' read than *What is Philosophy?*, nor that it provides a kind of heuristic algorithm, which, industriously applied, would allow us to reduce the difficulty and complexity of the original. Not a guide, and certainly not a substitute, it demands to be read alongside the text of Deleuze and Guattari; only thus can it perform the signal task of the commentary: to intensify the complexity of the text by selecting and modulating certain moments and perspectives within it, to reorient the reader by inflecting its topology and, most importantly, to spur the labour of new repetitions, new habitations of the text giving rise to novel connections and redistributions of its singular points. Unabashedly systemic, Deleuze and Guattari's philosophy is not by that token doctrinal, in the sense it would allow itself to be reduced or represented by a set of conveniently enumerable theses. The commentary, in this sense, is not a contribution to the construction of an orthodoxy, with all its attendant disciplinary effects, but a necessarily partial, perhaps partisan, effort to revitalize a philosophy, by a judicious combination of detailed excavation, on the one hand, and the potentially catalytic adjunction of new components, on the other.

Is it possible to write about a philosophy, without representing it, without reducing it to a set of easily registered and reproduced theses, gestures and applications? Or, to specify the question in terms of Deleuze and Guattari, if (their) philosophy is a theory of multiplicities, and the concept itself is best designated as an intensive or virtual multiplicity, is it at all warranted to treat their thought as a quantitative multiplicity, one that could be measured, divided and represented – or, to abide with our concern, expounded and introduced – without fundamentally changing its status? These doubts about representing an anti-representational thought should not in the least be confused with a crypto-theological injunction to silence, be it tragic, therapeutic or sublime – or worse, with a licence to indulge in pseudo-poetic effusions. On the contrary, besides the crucial conceptualization of the role of repetition in the history of philosophy, with which Alliez opens Chapter I and which is explored further in 'Deleuze Virtual Philosophy' (Appendix I), Deleuze provides us a fertile model for an other, non-representational and non-propositional, pedagogy when it comes to philosophers and their texts, what he calls *counter-actualization*. The 'ethics' of philosophy, the focus of the first Chapter of *The Signature of the World*, is not only the appraisal of systems of thought through the Spinozist lenses of pure immanence – the mobilization and perception of what Alliez calls 'the non-discursive auto-enunciation of the event' – it is also a matter of what it might mean to be 'worthy' of a philosophy in the same sense that Deleuze, in *The Logic of Sense*, spoke of being worthy of an event. To wrest Deleuze and Guattari from a synoptic regime of doctrinal introduction – the repetition that makes no difference – is also a question 'of becoming the quasi-cause of what is produced within us, the Operator; of producing surfaces and linings in which the event is reflected, finds itself again as incorporeal and manifests in us the neutral splendour which it possesses in itself in its impersonal and pre-individual nature, beyond the general and the particular, the collective and the private'. The commentator as quasi-cause or Operator of a philosophy, rather than the knowing purveyor of conceptual generalities that are as adequate to a sampled set of propositions as they are blind to the Event in or of a philosophy: here lies the role for philosophical commentary and philosophical history of the notion of the virtual. When it is not reified and spiritualized into standing for the mystical heart of production, the virtual allows us to delve into the specificity of philosophy as a kind of trans-historical machine for counter-actualization, which, instead of being tied to the constrictive and sterile parameters of objective or representational fidelity, tells us that the most 'constructed' of repetitions will also be the most expressive, that the most abstract will also be the most concrete, which is to say, it will be the commentary that goes deepest into the problematic field that generates the philosophical concepts which 'secondary literature' can only grasp as a static sequence of propositions. Whilst the latter is dead set on studiously actualizing a philosophy's problems into a digestible and well-ordered sequence of propositions, whose internal disparateness and heterogeneity has been thoroughly evacuated, the true commentary's task, again to quote *The Logic of Sense*, is 'to be the mime of *what effectively occurs*, to double the actualization with a counter-actualization, the identification with a distance, like the true actor and dancer, to give the truth

of the event the only chance of not being confused with its inevitable actualization. [. . .] To the extent that the pure event is each
time imprisoned forever in its actualization, counter-actualization liberates it, always for other times'. And, this being the interventionist and conjunctural character of the commentary, it
liberates it for *our* time, breathing life into the concept (and the
concept of the concept) by allowing it to resonate with components and virtualities outside of its domain of consistency.

All this is just by way of supporting evidence for the assertion
that philosophical pedagogy, as conceived by Deleuze and
Guattari and prolonged by Alliez, is necessarily a counter-
pedagogy, an ethics of philosophy and philosophical writing that
rejects the currently dominant picture according to which we
should aspire to an information transfer with the least possible
noise – a position this that happily ignores the Deleuzian redis-
tribution, again in *Difference and Repetition*, of the clear-and-
obscure over against the distinct-and-confused (the use of
Deleuze and Guattari as guarantors of a rhapsodic, sloganeer-
ing and awkwardly 'poetic' style is merely the counterpart of
such academicism, equally failing to attain the consistency of the
concept). Such a counter-pedagogy is intimately wedded to the
very distinctive concern with ontology, and more specifically
with 'onto-ethology', advocated by Alliez. Against the prepara-
tion of concepts for conspicuous consumption so prevalent
today, the aim of onto-ethology is instead to traverse, in order to
reactivate them, the singularities that compose a concept. This is
inevitably accompanied by a reinsertion of the concept – and in
particular the 'concept of the concept' advanced by Deleuze and
Guattari in *What is Philosophy?* – into the contemporary philosophical conjuncture, to elicit new interferences with the
domains of art and science. In this regard, there is no hard and
fast distinction between the prescriptive or interpretive concerns
we've been rehearsing up to now and the constructive and
expressive practice of philosophy itself. *What is Philosophy?*, as
read by Alliez, is emphatically not a meta-philosophical tract or
propaedeutic, but a bona fide ontological intervention, a potent
reconfiguration of philosophical practice inseparable from a
novel sequence of conceptual invention which, as Alliez shows,

namely with respect to the status of science and the appraisal of Bergsonism, both prolongs and transforms the collaborative work undertaken in the earlier *Capitalism and Schizophrenia* volumes. Given the equation of expressionism and constructivism that constitutes the privileged axis for Alliez's reading, we cannot sunder the affective and sensory qualities of the concept, of the concept as an inhabited, virtual reality, from its conditions of formation and transmission. If there is a privileged channel between art and philosophy it has to do with the former's capacity to mobilize and activate the sensible components of the concept, and thus to function as a possible catalyst or relay for philosophical activity itself.

Once again, the uniqueness of Alliez's text in the current panorama of presentations and interpretations is linked, despite its well-founded suspicion of any prescriptive methodological appropriation of Deleuze and Guattari, to its fidelity vis-à-vis the intimate link or even equation between the conditions of exercise of philosophical practice (which is to say, the parameters for the construction of concepts) and what we are often lazily led to consider as the 'claims' of a given philosophy. Onto-ethology rescinds the representational logic whereby such claims might try to legitimate themselves. It does so by elucidating how the practical immersion into concepts and their singularities (components) is not some supplementary epistemological exercise but rather lies at the very heart of ontology. Conversely, by drawing the consequences of the dismantling of the representational image of thought, with its connections to the static or quantitative multiplicities mentioned above, it circumvents the imperious demands of critique; if ontology as onto-ethology simply is the entry into the concept with its material resonances, its expressive potential, its non-philosophical outside – if the concept must perennially be reconstructed, differed in its repetition, linked to a perspective in and of the world – then we have abandoned any privileged vantage point that would allow us immanently to draw out the limits or boundaries of speculation and thereby attain the legislative eminence of meta-philosophy. The crucial lesson of *What is Philosophy?* then, as 'repeated' by Alliez, is precisely that any separation of ontological from expressive (and sensible) content, any sundering of philosophical 'statements' from their conditions of production, from the experience of construction, freezes philosophy into an easily manipulated, but ultimately lifeless, collection of propositions. By trying to attain the status of propositional knowledge, by trying to purify itself of the 'obscure' perceptive and affective components of the concept in the image of an impoverished, cleansed science, which is to say by severing its connections with art, philosophy would evacuate itself of its specificity, its attention to the life of the concept.

Alliez's relentless attention to the pedagogical link between the construction and expression of the concept, his raising of montage and style to matters of philosophical import, also leads him to provide a path through the thought of Deleuze and Guattari which, in its connections and consequences, goes against the grain of much of the diverse and often inconsistent (rather than positively meta-stable) field of 'Deleuzism' which has been gaining mass, if not momentum, in the years following the publication of *What is Philosophy?* This goes to demonstrate, if further demonstration were needed, that the pedagogical and presentational angle we've chosen to highlight is not the province of propaedeutic or meta-philosophical questions, but is endowed with all the speculative dignity and political charge of ontology, in its Spinozist incarnation. Two 'doctrinal' topics are most obviously affected by Alliez's traversal of *What is Philosophy?* It is worth dwelling on these at some length both to assay the considerable consequences of his particular portrait of the 'pedagogy of the concept' and to begin to imagine how such an intervention might help to reconfigure current debates and undermine a certain consensual reading of Deleuze (and Guattari) that currently seems to be making some headway. These two topics are the image of science, on the one hand, and the relation between ontology, phenomenology and aesthetics, on the other. Both, we shall argue, hinge on the status accorded to the notions of subjectivity and point of view (or perspective).

Much as the obvious sympathy displayed by Deleuze and Guattari toward certain currents in scientific theory might tempt us to align their project with some contemporary research programme – complexity theory being the most popular candidate these days – the speculative engagement with science in *What is Philosophy?*, reconstructed and expanded with considerable originality by Alliez, militates against any notion of a philosophy that would provide the ontological *supplement* for a given scientific theory, as much as it puts paid to the project of a critical eminence of philosophy over science. The passage from the perspective of critique to the project of ontogenesis and heterogenesis, from conditions of possible experience to conditions of real experience, signifies the relinquishing of any epistemological pretension, in full awareness that ontological scepticism, realism and their derivatives are hardly the urgent concern of today's science, with its surfeit of ideal-material entities, quasi-objects and quasi-subjects. Rather than trying to shore up a particular research programme or, vice versa, employ it to provide philosophical practice with some spurious legitimacy, *What is Philosophy?*, as traversed by Alliez, is preoccupied with delineating the constructive specificity of science, its manner of engaging with the chaos that beckons thought. It does this by focusing on individuation *in* science (of the states of things or affairs, of functions, limits and partial observers) and correlatively on the individuation of science – whence the seemingly paradoxical heading of Chapter 2, 'The Aetiology of Science' – against the objectivist ontology that pervades the determinist or mechanist tradition. Such a tradition, according to Alliez's account, is wedded to the essentially transcendent – because non-relational and force-free – individuation of non-partial observers; there is thus a correspondence between the view from nowhere of the *scientia dei* and the abstract ontology of the object, which only an attention to the problematic and polemical constitution of scientific objectivity can undermine. It is this joint conception of the heterogenesis of thought and the ontogenesis of being that represents the hallmark of what Deleuze and Guattari in *Anti-Oedipus* term transcendental materialism. To regard the latter as the ontology of a given scientific approach would be to ignore that the 'image of science' outlined in *What is Philosophy?* is a construction produced from within philosophy and its history, specifically against *mathesis universalis*, Laplacean determinism,

and the physics of states, rather than a kind of ideological supplement or support for a particular scientific theory.

At the opposite and complementary extreme of the proto-
analytic and post-positivistic take on the relation between philosophy and science is the creeping tendency to elide the 'new
materialism' of Deleuze and Guattari with the various phenom-
enologies of embodiment that take Merleau-Ponty as their principal referent. The originality of Alliez's stance in this respect lies,
first, in reading the confrontation with aesthetics in *What is
Philosophy?* (which prolongs Deleuze's work in *The Logic of
Sense* and *Francis Bacon: The Logic of Sensation*) as an effective
refutation of any confusion between the thinking of the Body
without Organs and the Merleau-Pontyian concern with the
flesh; second, in identifying the passage to a materialist phenomenology of the concept as the best antidote to the ambient pieties
of intentional consciousness and its collapse into absolute alterity (Levinas) or spiritualist immanence (Michel Henry) – 'a
phenomenology of the concept to put an end to all phenome-
nologies', as Alliez writes in *De l'impossibilité de la phénoménologie*. The indissoluble link between the pre-individual character of
sensibility and affect and the unabashed artificiality of artistic
invention, taken as the prism through which to grasp the singularity of contemporary art, is thus employed against any notion
of art as the site of a manifestation of subjectivity. Whilst the elic-
iting of certain figures of subjectivity from the capture of chaos
in assemblages of percepts and affects is certainly not to be dis-
counted, the consistency of the artwork cannot be simply
enveloped in a perceiving subject without lopping off one of the
two halves of aesthetics (sensation and experiment, passivity and
artifice) which Deleuze so insistently endeavoured to think
together. From this standpoint, that of 'the sensible idea of a
material indiscernibility between Art and Life', phenomenology
'denatures' the plane of immanence by forcing life into the con-
fines of a teleologically ordered subjectivity, commanded by the
principles of good sense and common sense. Concurring with
Badiou's polemical characterization of Deleuze's project in his
review of *The Fold*, though reversing the verdict, Alliez identifies
the wager of this philosophy in the notion of a self-description of

Life in a 'virtual phenomenology of the concept' as experience and experiment (whence the characterization of Deleuze's philosophy as a transcendental empiricism). The term phenomenology, of course, is used in the most provocative of guises, since the notion of description is here divorced from any figure of subjective interiority, intentionality or embodiment. The 'self' in self-description indicates a kind of torsion or fold of the plane of immanence in the fractured individuality of the philosopher (*Difference and Repetition*) and the self-positing of the concept (*What is Philosophy?*). However, against the circulating opinion that notions of subjectivity are simply alien to Deleuze's (and Guattari's) philosophy, Alliez, following the entire thematic of the 'brain' in *What is Philosophy?* and the arguments of shorter texts such as 'The Conception of Difference in Bergson', 'How Do We Recognize Structuralism?', 'Immanence: A Life . . .' or 'The Actual and the Virtual', does allow us to move toward a novel, Deleuzian conception of subjectivity no longer wedded to the Cartesian subject of knowledge or the phenomenological subject of perception. Whence the importance of the Leibnizian discussion of Whitehead in *What is Philosophy?*, where the 'question is no longer that of the methodological dependence of the object in relation to the subject, but of the ontological auto-constitution of a new subject on the basis of its objects'. Following Whitehead, the subject (or rather 'superject') arises from the prehension of its world, meaning that the ontology of the sensible is not separable from the constitution of material processes and assemblages themselves. This neo-Leibnizian philosophy of subjectivation also provides speculative support for the thesis that contemporary art does not provide a site for the reflection of a pre-existing phenomenological subject but elicits the machinic production of new subjects, new fulcrums of prehension. The humanist telos of the phenomenology of perception, always more or less implicitly bound to the 'proper function' of embodiment, is dissolved by an experimentation with the senses that doubles the constructivism of the concept. A constructivism that is not so distant from the kind articulated by the great Soviet director and constructivist Dziga Vertov, when he wrote in 1923: 'The mechanical eye, the camera, rejecting the human eye as crib sheet, gropes its way through the chaos of visual events, letting itself be drawn or repelled by movement, probing, as it goes, the path of its own movement. It experiments, distending time, dissecting movement or, in contrary fashion, absorbing time within itself, swallowing years, thus schematizing processes of long duration inaccessible to the normal eye.'

In a review greeting the appearance of *What is Philosophy?*, Antonio Negri spoke of that book as the first philosophical system of the twenty-first century, 'a common philosophy alternative to capitalist modernity. In its rigorous materialism it presents itself as a common philosophy, in its instance of absolute immanence it liquidates the postmodern'. Also ascribing to the thesis of a turn away from foundationalism but toward ontology, instead of hermeneutics, Alliez himself rehearses a variety of appellations to capture the uniqueness of Deleuze and Guattari's approach: metaphysical materialism, ontology of the virtual, empiricism as speculative materialism, a *finally* revolutionary philosophical materialism, Ideal-materialism of the pure event, experimental naturalism, practical vitalism, ontology of experience, virtual phenomenology of the concept. We could even say that one of the principal aims of these commentaries and variations on the difference of Deleuze and Guattari's philosophy is to displace the commonplace assurances that still permeate philosophical discourse about terms such as idealism, realism, naturalism, phenomenology and, above all, materialism. As we have seen, Alliez suggests that philosophical materialism need not entail a subservience to some variety of scientific realism (whether deterministic or otherwise) and that, through an attention to the processual, expressive and constructive character of contemporary art, it can also present itself as a 'material meta-aesthetics'. In this regard, Deleuze and Guattari's philosophy is portrayed as a hitherto unheard of convergence of an ontology of 'fluid and crystalline' matter, as the site of processes of assemblage and individuation, and a thinking of practice which encompasses a range of activities from conceptual construction to political organization. The separation within materialism of a determinist or mechanist tendency, on the one hand, and a philosophy of praxis or 'materialism without matter' (to quote

Balibar), on the other, is diagonally undermined by a thinking of the heterogenesis of both material density and subjective action from a pre-individual field, divergently accessed by philosophy, science and art. It is here that the equation of expressionism and constructivism – inasmuch as 'expression is the constitutive activity of being' – is doubled by the indiscernibility of experience and experiment, such that material individuation and conceptual invention can be thought on the same plane. This also explains why, against both the phenomenology of intentional consciousness and the determinist thinking of a lifeless matter, Alliez sustains the thesis – based on a theoretical lineage that includes Leibniz, Tarde and Whitehead – that it is only by resuscitating, within the context of contemporary science, a certain perspectivism or pan-psychism that one can really be faithful to materialism, a materialism for which matter turns into a sensed-sensing energy with multiple centres, foldings or perspectives that precede the formation of measured and measuring subjects. Or, to slightly change register, any naturalism that doesn't prioritize *natura naturans* (the pre-individual) over *natura naturata* (the individuated) will remain a thinking of possible rather than real experience.

But what is perhaps most significant about Alliez's operation, and what might also account for the scanty attention given to *What is Philosophy?* by most Deleuzians, is the absolute centrality he accords to the question of *thought*, which he places at the very heart of Deleuze and Guattari's recasting of materialism for the twenty-first century as a materialism of the concept. For *What is Philosophy?* clearly shows that it is impossible to answer the question without also expanding it to 'What is Thought?' and to the conflicts, interactions and interferences between philosophy and non-philosophical thought, as well as between thought and the tendencies and transformations that traverse the contemporary world. In a sentence that perhaps best encapsulates the crux of his project, Alliez writes: 'In *practice*, the question is that of a theory of thought capable of diagnosing in our becomings the ontological conditions for the real experience of thought.' These ontological conditions are therefore not invariant schemas of possibility, but the consequence of real transformations in the problematic fields or abstract machines that engender our actual predicament and our philosophical legacy. The practical and interventionist (or polemical) impetus of this kind of enquiry cannot be ignored; constructivism cannot do without the insertion of ontology into a present state of affairs and the counter-actualization of this state of affairs through a sensitivity to the event and its material repercussions. This is why 'thought only says what it is by saying what it does' ('Deleuze Virtual Philosophy', Proposition I). Eschewing an interrogation of this anti-epistemological and non-rationalist theory of thought as a practice of invention and counter-actualization, most treatments of Deleuze and Guattari have either reduced their philosophy to a kind of dogmatism that represents matter in a set of theses regarding its flux-like nature, its dynamism, its processes of stratification and . . . its non-representable character; or sutured it (to paraphrase Badiou) to a condition (be it science, art or politics), which is no longer a condition of real experience but more like a pretext. Whence the use of certain artistic products or movements as illustrations of a putative Deleuzo-Guattarian doctrine or the depiction of a given research programme as the experimental extension of their materialist ontology. In both instances, we lose the specificity of philosophical practice, together with its articulation and sometimes polemical discontinuity with regard to other forms of thought, turning the risky ethics and ethology of thought into a pacifying ideology: the paradoxical representation, rather than real repetition, of a thought without an image. Where the thinking of Deleuze and Guattari is often reduced to an updated variant of classical materialism, an adjunct to new scientific models or a less Christian branch of phenomenology, Alliez, armed with the insights of Neo-Platonism, Bergsonism and Tardean monadology, points to 'the speculative identity of a philosophy of intuition and a philosophy of the concept', manifested in the turn from essence to ethology, as being the hallmark of this philosophical system for the twenty-first century.

If the 'involuntary adventure' of culture, as Deleuze notes, is what allows us to 'penetrate the coloured thickness of a problem,' *l'épaisseur colorée d'un problème*, we can only hope that *The Signature of the World* will contribute, against the compulsory generation of slogans and facile certainties – what *Difference and Repetition* decried as 'the grotesque image of culture that we find in examinations and government referenda' – to making more acute the problematic character of Deleuze and Guattari's work, which, conceived as an intensive multiplicity in its own right, as a system in heterogenesis, demands the creativity of commentary rather than the sterile tedium of exposition.

A.T.
Tehran, April 2004

Notes and Acknowledgements

This translation would never have left my Paris room, which was only matched in windowlessness by the state of my mind, without the immense labours of Alberto Toscano; who, with extraordinary patience, not only dragged pieces of the manuscript out of me when I must have been one of the most unreachable, reluctant, reticent, and disengaged of translators, but also, tracked down references, filled in the bits of the original French that I found utterly impenetrable, and ultimately ensured that this book came into existence. Matteo Mandarini offered me his indefatigable support in numerous ways throughout the period in which this translation was undertaken. Finally, I owe gratitude beyond measure to my parents, brother, cat, and the handful of friends – they know who they are – who doggedly stuck by me whilst I journeyed through what Judge Schreber would have described as 'a holy time'.

E.R.A.

I have tried, as far as possible, not to encumber the text with too many bracketed insertions of the original French terms, choosing to do so only when it seemed strictly necessary from the standpoint of conceptual precision. Though specific issues of translation are dealt with individually in the notes, it is worth indicating that I was led, in dialogue with the author, to make some choices that go against the now established translations of the works of Deleuze and Guattari. Most significantly, in order to maintain its important difference from 'sensation' and 'perception', which is generally elided in extant translations, I have chosen to render *le sensible*, in the sense of 'that which can be sensed', simply as 'the sensible', despite the awkwardness of expression that this might occasionally entail.

Page references in parentheses are to *Qu'est-ce que la philosophie* (Paris: Minuit, 1991) and *What is philosophy?*, trans. Graham Burchell and Hugh Tomlinson (London: Verso, 1994) – in that order. Some translations have been modified for greater accuracy or harmony with Alliez's text. References in the form 'I, 1' relate to the part and chapter of the book respectively. All footnotes in brackets are the translators'.

I wish to thank Keith Ansell Pearson, Ray Brassier, John Sellars, and Damian Veal for their timely help with locating references and translations, Stephen Zepke for reading through the final manuscript, and Hywel Evans, Sarah Douglas and Anya Wilson at Continuum. I would also like to thank Éric Alliez for his extensive collaboration on the final revision of the manuscript.

A.T.

This work was initially conceived with Isabelle Stengers. Geographical distance and the complexity of the questions posed by *What is Philosophy?* conspired in preventing us from seeing our collaborative project through to its completion. Suffice it to say that her name continues to circulate in the ellipsis of discovery and invention which both anticipated and revived this *different* text presented here under a single signature. A text that would perhaps never have turned into a book were it not for the friendly insistence of Danielle Cohen-Levinas. And the death of Félix Guattari.

E.A.

To Félix,
the smile of the Cheshire cat

Introduction

Ir, ir indo
Caetano Veloso

What is Philosophy? Through the reserve of immanence of the
event it constitutes, this book, the last to bear Deleuze and
Guattari's joint signature, imposes a veritable ascesis upon the
reader, who is summoned to project himself into a becoming he
can never be sure will be his own: Has the time come for this
reader to ask what philosophy is, and to speak concretely? A time
when asking what philosophy is no longer represents a stylistic
exercise or an act of reflection; when one reaches that 'point of
nonstyle where one can finally say, "What is it I have been doing
all my life?"' (7/1). Like a past tense rising up into the present,
are these first lines not the best index of our inexorable inade-
quacy when confronted by the task to let go of doing (too much)
philosophy?

　All that's left for the reader is to become the artisan of his own
reading, step by step, and to do so, if needs be, by multiplying
marginalia: that will then be the guiding principle of this *commentary effect*, like a notebook whose haphazard composition
prevents us from distinguishing the *cum* of 'commentator' from
the *inter* of 'interpreter'. In a word, what is required is an intervention. For it is the strength and the paradox of this book that
it forces us to carry out an exercise in 'textual commentary' in
order to escape both the fatality of Exegesis and the snare of

Reference. At a remove from any epiphany of sense, it is a question here of a pedagogy of immanence that will make us follow, rather than reproduce, the question of philosophy in the urgency of its rivalry with modern science – even if this entails that, in the course of this confrontation, science may discover its links with a processual paradigm traditionally ascribed to 'art'.

Though we have to wait until midnight to ask this question, Deleuze and Guattari's midnight designates the longest day. The sun of the midnight when one will pose the question of philosophy like a confidence amongst friends, a confidence tantamount to a challenge against an enemy, whose nature (The Great Communicator) obliges us to distrust even the friend. It is a moment when the contingency of the reasons behind the invention and reinvention of this singular exercise of thought called 'philosophy' is illuminated from the perspective, both oblique and non-destinal, of an 'absolute disaster': the disaster of *logical possibility as philosophical impossibility.** A moment when the answer must escape the sovereign cliché of the question, in order to determine 'an hour, an occasion, some circumstances, some landscapes and personae, some conditions and unknowns of the question' (8/2).

In *practice*, the question is that of a theory of thought capable of diagnosing in our becomings the ontological conditions for the real experience of thought.

---

* (POST-)ANALYTICAL NOTE 1: 'What do you mean by these statements?' This interpellation of the 'metaphysician', with its policeman's tone, governs what is usually referred to as the *Manifesto of the Vienna Circle*: R. Carnap, H. Hahn and O. Neurath, *Wissenschaftliche Weltauffassung: Der Wiener Kreis* (Vienna: Artur Wolf Verlag, 1929); 'The Scientific Conception of the World: The Vienna Circle', trans. P. Foulkes and M. Neurath, in Otto Neurath, *Empiricism and Sociology*, eds. M. Neurath and R.S. Cohen (Dordrecht and Boston: Reidel, 1973), pp. 299–318. This text sets out a programme aimed at establishing a 'total system of concepts', that can be 'grasped intersubjectively' (p. 306) by way of logical analysis (or 'logistics') and 'tautological transformation' (p. 308). In that way, 'the clarification of the traditional philosophical problems leads us partly to unmask them as pseudo-problems and partly to transform them into empirical problems and thereby to subject them to the judgement of experimental science' (p. 306). Rorty's commentary on this question is a fine example of 'reflexive equilibrium': 'This is close to Heidegger's own meaning, as is shown by the fact that some of his examples of pseudo-problems

(POST-)ANALYTICAL NOTE 1: (*continued*)
("other minds," "the external world") are the same as Carnap's' (Richard Rorty, 'Philosophy as Science, as Metaphor, and as Politics', in *Essays on Heidegger and others, Philosophical Papers vol. II* [Cambridge: Cambridge University Press, 1991], p. 17). In this respect, we are not so far from Deleuze either, since a pseudo-problem only ever focuses on a difference that '*makes* no difference'. Here is another *post-analytical* commentary, by Putnam: '[What were] called "attacks on metaphysics" [. . .] were amongst the most ingenious, profound, and technically brilliant constructions of metaphysical systems ever achieved. Even if they failed [Charles Larmore has suggested the word *autocritique*], modern symbolic logic, a good deal of modern language theory, and a part of contemporary cognitive science were all offshoots of these attempts.' (Hilary Putnam, 'After Empiricism' [1984], in *Realism with a Human Face* [Cambridge, MA: Harvard University Press, 1990], p. 52). We could add here, to quote the title of another article by Rorty, 'The Priority of Democracy to Philosophy', which contributes to making *essentially* unquestionable – in the sense of pragmatically impertinent – what he calls 'postmodern bourgeois liberalism'. In brief, *if there is no other game in town*, the analytic style, like 'democracy', would represent the lesser evil . . . On the proto-positivism of the *Rorty Roller*, see Richard Bernstein, 'One Step Forward, Two Steps Backward: Rorty on Liberal Democracy and Philosophy', in *Political Theory* 15/4 (November 1987), pp. 538–63, and Roy Bhaskar, *Philosophy and the Idea of Freedom* (Blackwell: Oxford, 1991). (The first two quotations were originally taken from Jacques Bouveresse, 'Une différence sans distinction', *Philosophie* 35 [Summer 1992], pp. 70–1.)

I   The *Ethics* of Philosophy

The first man ever to have posed the problem of reading,
and in consequence, of writing, was Spinoza . . .
Louis Althusser, *Reading Capital*

'As I say, I didn't understand every word but when you're dealing
with such ideas you feel as though you were taking a witch's ride.
After that I wasn't the same man.' Having at some point or other
been swept away like this himself, every reader of Deleuze should
know that these lines from Bernard Malamud's *The Fixer* – that
relate the protagonist's discovery of Spinoza and are reproduced
at the beginning of *Spinoza: Practical Philosophy* – could serve
equally well as an introduction to the essentially Deleuzian question of the *philosophical sense* of the history of philosophy.
Difference and Repetition, *The Logic of Sense*: it is under this
double heading that the dazzling play of conceptual variation
elicited by the monographic analysis of the early works – works
where everything already tended towards the 'great identity'
Spinoza-Nietzsche – will be taken up again and thought through
as such. Spinoza filtered through Cervantes, Borges through
Bergson; Nietzsche, unfastened from Heidegger, meets Lewis
Carroll before being delivered over to the becomings-animal of
his 'poietic' metamorphoses. The concept thus becomes narrative and philosophy a new genre of story in which description
takes the place of the object, in which the point of view replaces
the subject – the subject of enunciation and of disfigurement.

What Deleuze said of the Baroque[1] brings us back, as it were, to the scene of the crime:

> The history of philosophy is the reproduction of philosophy itself. In the history of philosophy, a commentary should act as a veritable double and bear the maximal modification appropriate to a double. It should be possible to recount a real book of past philosophy as if it were an imaginary and feigned book. In this case the most exact, the most strict repetition has as its correlate the maximum of difference [. . .] Commentaries in the history of philosophy should represent a kind of slow motion, a congelation or immobilisation of the text: *not only* of the text to which they relate, *but also* of the text in which they are inserted – so much so that they have a double existence and a corresponding ideal: the pure repetition of the former text [*texte ancien*] and the present text [*texte actuel*] in *one another*.[2]

Difference and repetition as the logic of sense, constitution of the difference of sense, *narration* of the concept and of the adventures of sense – Deleuze has never ceased proposing descriptive notions that participate in a *phantastique* of the imagination. Multiplying the Examples in the guise of brief reviews, alternating and mixing together, on the one hand, the infinite speeds of thought in its becoming and, on the other, the slowing down of the historical exposition of concepts as a function of the problems to which they respond; taking on, as an explicit task, a *pedagogy of the concept* (17/12), which, in Part One of the book ('Philosophy'), will tend to turn the history of philosophy into a *philosophy of philosophy*[3] and to produce the concept of the concept – *What is Philosophy?* lays out the

[1] Gilles Deleuze, *Le Pli. Leibniz et le Baroque* (Paris: Minuit, 1988), p. 174; *The Fold: Leibniz and the Baroque*, trans. Tom Conley (Minneapolis: University of Minnesota Press, 1993), p. 127. [It is from this same passage that Alliez takes the title of the present book. As Deleuze writes, 'Leibniz's philosophy must be conceived as the allegory of the world, the signature of the world.']

[2] Preface to Gilles Deleuze, *Différence et Répétition* (Paris: PUF, 1968), pp. 4–5; *Difference and Repetition*, trans. Paul Patton (London: Athlone Press, 1994), p. xxi.

[3] In Wilhelm Dilthey's phrase, from his *Weltanschauungslehre. Abhandlungen zur Philosophie der Philosophie*, *Gesammelte Schriften*, Band VIII, ed. B. Groethuysen (Göttingen: Vandenhoeck & Rupert, 1991).

balance sheet and programme of a philosophical life. Written, of necessity, with Félix Guattari, that is, on the basis of a truly philosophical necessity, this final book also inscribes itself, and inevitably so, within the movement of *Capitalism and Schizophrenia*. What is the history of philosophy, if not a 'geophilosophy' and a speculative cartography of the milieus and rhythms of thought (I, 4)?

In the first slowing down, we encounter Descartes. Or, more precisely, the Cartesian *cogito* since, both in the first Examples (1 through 5) and in the text itself, the *cogito* 'doubles' what, for us moderns, counts as a beginning in philosophy. There is no need here to quote Schelling, Hegel, Husserl or Heidegger: it is starting from Descartes that the history to which we belong (i.e. the 'present text') poses the question of philosophy and subordinates its exercise to that 'singular point where concept and creation are related to each other' (16/11). The singularity of the Cartesian point of departure is that it makes beginning into such a determinant problem that it ends up directly relating the question of beginning to the problem of philosophy. This point of departure is modern inasmuch as the relation between philosophy and beginning must be posed to the exclusion of 'any explicit objective presupposition where every concept refers to other concepts' (31/26). This means that from now on the only presuppositions will be implicit and subjective and a pre-philosophical comprehension will be the sole arbiter over access to the new philosophical regime (whence the *Metaphysical Meditations*). 'So the problem is: "What is the first concept on this plane or, by beginning with what concept, can truth as absolutely pure subjective certainty be determined?" Such is the cogito.' Such is the Cartesian plane, the single plane on the basis of which the 'other concepts will be able to achieve objectivity, but only if they are linked by bridges to the first concept, if they respond to problems subject to the same conditions and if they remain on the same plane. Objectivity here will assume a certainty of knowledge rather than presuppose a truth recognized as preexisting, or already there' (31/27).

Why start the series of reviews, or Examples, with Descartes?

At the end of this first survey [*survol*] of the Cartesian plane, the reader is faced with a twofold answer. To begin with, we can remark that the creation of the concept of cogito refers back to a *pre-philosophical intuition*, which it presupposes to the same degree it is conditioned by it. Descartes's genius can thus be seen to lie in the manner he explores and restores in the first person ('I') this non-conceptual comprehension (which is subjective and implicit: like a perception or a *percept* extricated from all discursive elements) 'is perhaps closer to the heart of philosophy than philosophy itself'. In other words, Descartes *realizes* that 'philosophy defined as the creation of concepts implies a presupposition which distinguishes itself from concepts but is nevertheless inseparable from them' (43/41). This is what Deleuze and Guattari, resuming an operation already amply developed in *A Thousand Plateaus*, call the *plane of immanence* (I, 2), or the 'image of thought' (according to another expression, which refers in turn to *Difference and Repetition*): I who doubt, cannot doubt that I think; or, alternatively, the image of what thinking signifies: I think, therefore I am. The singular aspect of this affair, in which the Cogito-effect comes to be defined, is that what everyone knows (what it means to doubt, to think, to be) will be selected as thought's rightful object; in being so selected, thought becomes the object of its own movement, insofar as this movement can be carried to infinity.

This movement of the infinite is only thinkable (or conceivable) in turn inasmuch as it puts the very horizon (of thought) in motion: this is what defines both the immanence of the plane *and* the (infinite) movement of thought as 'a coming and going, because it does not advance toward a destination without already turning back on itself, the needle also being the pole' (40/38). That is why the lightning flash of thought is a double blow, once *infinite movement is not the image of thought without also returning as the matter of being*. It is thus that in the Cartesian perspective of classical modernity, there is no longer any being which is not *de jure* thinkable (*cogitabile*). In other words, it is once again with Descartes that the idea that the *most subjective will be the most objective* falls into the categories of representation. As Deleuze and Guattari write: 'the concept posits itself to the same extent that it is created' (16/11) – i.e. self-positing [*autoposition*].

Postulating the 'I think' as an autoposition of the self is obviously not a matter of 'method', but rather an experimentation whose immanent conditions, which are not themselves immediately discursive, establish the deterritorialized 'plan(e)' [*plan*] of enunciation. But this plane, which depends upon the 'deterritorialisation of existential territories' (Guattari), can be laid out only if one is first able to impose a certain curvature upon the infinite speeds that compose the mental chaos into which thought has plunged. Even Descartes has his dream, the 'witch's flight' (44/41) which escaped the cauldron and led him to make his own chaos. This dream is the hyperbolic doubt or 'chaoticizing' chaos; a schizo-chaotic – rather than phenomenological – reduction, which 'undoes every consistency in the infinite' and marks 'the impossibility of a relation between two determinations' (44–5/42). But strange personae now begin to emerge onto the plane of immanence: first comes the Idiot, who'll doubt everything by dint of wanting to think everything for himself; then the Evil Demon [*Malin Génie*], who insists we cast doubt upon everything so that he can appropriate for himself the power of the infinite, which he hurls at whatever itself insists. And finally, in spite of the authors' warnings,[4] what are we to say about the Cartesian God, this creator of eternal verities who is only opposed to the 'trickster God' [*Dieu trompeur*] by virtue of his own goodness and truthfulness? So many *conceptual personae* (I, 3), so many enunciatory folds forcing a variation to the infinite, so many sections of chaos acting like sieves that restore an

---

[4] Another difference between science and philosophy could be discerned in the fact that, *under certain conditions*, God can become as 'singular' as a conceptual persona . . . For their part, Deleuze and Guattari write the following: 'the fact that [in science] there is no total observer [. . .] means only that God is no more a scientific observer than he is a philosophical persona' (122/129). Descartes could well be the *exception* that *proves* the rule, to the extent that he is almost alone in refusing to judge the wisdom of God according to the standards of mathematical omnipotence. As Schelling remarked, that is how 'philosophy entered its second childhood' – a childhood that, as Jean-Luc Marion stresses, is as provisional as it is untenable (*Sur la théologie blanche de Descartes* [Paris: PUF, 1981], pp. 452–3). As for the Spinozist *deus sive natura*, it *functions* as an abstract machine for the capitalization of processual powers.

operational narrativity and an existential alterity to speculation. They 'carry out the movements that describe the author's plane of immanence, and play a part in the very creation of the author's concepts. [. . .] The conceptual persona is the becoming or the subject of a philosophy, on a par with the philosopher [. . .]. I am no longer myself but thought's aptitude for finding itself and spreading across a plane that passes through me at several places' (62–3/63–4).

Let thought become *ethos* – and Descartes will never be quite the same . . .[5] For how are we to conceive (clearly and distinctly) the *methodical* deduction of concepts on the basis of the plane without the *events of thought* to which conceptual personae lend their sensible traits? It is only from the 'affective' and 'perceptual' *point of view* of the conceptual persona that the plane can be traced and concepts can be created on the plane of immanence. It took an Idiot to discover the ever-renewed movement of thought intuited by Descartes *qua* event, bringing together in a single notion the three phases of a variation in which all the components of the *concept 'cogito'* (I'-doubting, I''-thinking, I'''-being) end up coinciding.

So we will not affirm of the concept that it unveils the essence or sense of the thing. Rather, the concept states a part of the event that has taken place upon the plane. Moreover, it is as (dated) event that the (signed) concept is a multiplicity, comprising a finite number of components that, in turn, are traversed by the 'conceptual point' which never stops 'rising and falling within them. In this sense, each component is an *intensive feature* . . .' (25/20). I'- I''- I'''
. . . If the life of the concept is made up of these variations, its consistency – and hence its definition – is given by the inseparability of 'heterogeneous components traversed by a point of absolute survey [*un point en survol absolu*] at infinite speed' (26/21).

If it is still too soon to grasp the heterogenesis of this definition (of the concept as heterogenesis) – since we attain here the maximal modification aimed at by the pure repetition of the former (Cartesian) text and the present (Deleuzo-Guattarian) one, the one in the other – at least we can try to draw nearer to

[5] See Félix Guattari, *Chaosmose* (Paris: Galilée, 1992), p. 116.

what makes the Cartesian *self* [*moi*] exemplary from the point of
view of a constructivism that grasps philosophy through a
double operation: to create (philosophical) concepts, to trace a
(pre-conceptual) plane. To sum it up in a formula: the enunciation of self-positing (I think, therefore . . .) is strictly immanent
to the creation of the concept of the cogito (. . . I am), since, far
from any objective or transcendent presupposition, its 'sole
object is the inseparability of the components that constitute its
consistency and through which it passes back and forth' (28/23).
Moreover, if there exists a concept with no reference other than
itself, it is surely the *cogito* – Example 1, or the first repetition of
the former text: 'self-referential; it posits itself and its object at
the same time as it is created' (27/22).

QED? Not exactly, since, as enunciated by Deleuze and
Guattari, the above formulation applies *of course* to *every
concept*. Moreover, the difficulty is multiplied, owing to the fact
that it is *also* with and ever since Descartes that immanence
encounters the modern formula of its categorical reversal:
immanence is immanent *to* a pure consciousness. This formula
immediately reintroduces the transcendent (47/44–5),[6] in the
guise of an ego-onto-theology whose scansion *stops the movement* of self-positing and self-reference in order to re-establish
the rightful claims of natural theology and rational psychology;
and, furthermore, to inscribe into the identity of the concept the
obligations of a *mathesis universalis*, in which the reality of every
res will be founded *in quantum mensuratum et ordinatum* in its
relation to the *ego*. (Here we can perceive *a contrario* that reference 'concerns not the Event but rather a relationship with a
state of affairs or body and with the conditions of this relationship' [27/22].) But doesn't this mean, inversely, that in its difference every concept is self-referential, to the extent that *one does*

[6] [The importance of this line of argument to Deleuze and Guattari's critique
of those philosophies that claim to be either materialist or immanent, but that
only succeed, by a series of equivalent moves, in surreptitiously reintroducing
transcendence, cannot be overstressed: 'Whenever immanence is interpreted as
immanent "to" something [. . .] the concept becomes a transcendent universal
[. . .] we can be sure that this Something reintroduces the transcendent'
(47/44–5).]

not stop the infinite movement of thought, the movement that produces the necessity of the concept and 'takes it back to the open
sea' (196/208)? In other words, that thought turns on itself until
it has dragged into its orbit the very question of philosophy: '*To
give consistency without losing anything of the infinite*' (45/42) . . .

It is now – a 'now' tantamount to an 'always'[7] – that the former
text comes to insert itself in the present one, giving rise to the
greatest difference: 'and there is Philosophy whenever there is
immanence' (46/43). This is why philosophy, in its infinite
becoming, does not merge with its own history; rather, the
history of philosophy is like the hypertext wherein the affirmation of immanence and the illusion of transcendence are perpetually facing off.

But there remains the savage anomaly: Spinoza, or the 'infinite
becoming-philosopher' (59/60).

That is because, for Deleuze (and Guattari), no one better than
Spinoza showed what are the conditions of constructivism *qua*
real experience of thought. Spinoza's 'strange privilege' and the
mystery surrounding that 'something that no one else seems to
have succeeded at [. . .] a philosopher with an extraordinary conceptual apparatus, extremely directed, systematic and scholarly;
and yet he is the quintessential object of an immediate, unpre-
pared encounter, such that a non-philosopher or even someone
without any formal education, can receive from him a sudden
illumination, a "flash"'.[8] The flash of Spinoza, the man from
Kiev . . .

Under these conditions, it is hard to see how the secret of
Spinozism could fail to transpire at the very level of the principle governing the definitions of the *Ethics* and their concatenation. We must beware of calling these definitions 'genetic' (thus
risking a confusion of Spinoza with Hobbes) without adding at

[7] In Deleuze that is, since the *descriptive notions* he incessantly proposes all
begin by describing the setting in movement of the 'sedentary' categories to
which they were counter-posed.

[8] Gilles Deleuze, *Spinoza: Philosophie pratique* (Paris: Minuit, 1981), p. 173;
Spinoza: Practical Philosophy, trans. Robert Hurley (San Francisco: City Lights
Books, 1988), p. 129.

once that they only hold to the extent they express and reveal the inner movement of the 'thing' *together with what the thing itself allows us to perceive* – i.e. the thing's energetic power [*puissance*] and its effect of ontological discursiveness. In this regard, Spinozist definitions do not derive from a reflexive relationship of the representer to the represented that would necessarily transcend them (as their reference); rather, they manifest an *expressive material aspect* immanent to their conditions of enunciation. Regarding definitions, we could repeat what Deleuze says about Ideas, to wit that they 'do indeed "represent" some thing, but they represent a thing precisely because they "express" their own cause', as well as what he says about Attributes, that they are 'dynamic and active forms'.[9] Definitions are not, therefore, representations, endowed with the supplementary dimension of redoubling that representation implies – *a plan(e) of transcendence* – but rather affirmations, *auto-objective expressions* entering into internal relations that constitute so many 'foldings' on the plane of immanence, conferring upon determinability its dimension of 'interiority' in conformity with the infinite mode of essence. By vectorizing matters of expression rather than (always) already formed contents, the principle or plane of composition will be perceived simultaneously with what it composes, in the ontological identity of the form of expression and the form of content.[10]

In this regard, it would not be entirely illegitimate to speak of *pseudo-definitions*.[11] We need to recall here that the perspective of constitution, which is inseparable from Spinozist constructivism,

[9] Gilles Deleuze, *Spinoza et le problème de l'expression* (Paris: Minuit, 1968), pp. 124 and 36; *Expressionism in Philosophy: Spinoza*, trans. Martin Joughin (New York: Zone Books, 1992), pp. 138 and 45.

[10] One could easily show that Guattari's schizoanalytic cartographies partake, *via* Hjelmslev, in a veritable Spinozism of the unconscious. Concerning Hjelmslev, Guattari says that 'he produced a kind of Spinozist theory of language'.

[11] Particularly suggestive in this respect is Wolff's critical reading of Spinozism in his *Theologia naturalis*. Wolff notes that even though the sole criterion of truth is logical coherence, Spinoza is still satisfied with pseudo-evidences, which he arbitrarily names 'definitions'. His conclusion is the following: Spinoza's God is so different from that of Christianity that the only thing they have in common is their name, which Spinoza could have done without . . .

employs a geometrical mode of exposition only then to subordinate it to a dynamism whose character is more biological, or
physico-chemical, than properly mathematical. (Herein lies the
importance of the introduction of 'common notions', which is
not devoid of repercussions for the entire ontological project of
the *Ethics*, since it is by their intermediation that being affirms
itself practically – in its constitution – as an assemblage of relations capable of entering into composition).[12] That is why
Spinozist 'definitions' are geometric only in accordance with a
natural geometry, which introduces the life of nature such as it is
effectuated in the absolute that expresses it (the expressive nature
of the absolute). The perfection of Spinoza's plane of immanence is nothing but the outcome of this *immediate, perpetual,
instantaneous exchange*, of this *reversibility* of 'the immanence of
expression in what expresses itself and of what is expressed in its
expression'[13] – an exchange whereby *there is only a fold between
the one and the other*. To put it otherwise, in an extremely simple
formula: Spinoza 'produced the movement of the infinite'
(49/48); 'the greatest philosophers are hardly more than apostles
who distance themselves from or draw near to this mystery. [. . .]
Thus Spinoza is the Christ of philosophers' (59/60). *What is
Philosophy?*, if not the Imitation of Spinoza and the expression-
ist meditation of the constructivism of the *Ethics* . . .[14]

The *Ethics* OF philosophy then, if learning to philosophize
amounts to knowing how to perceive that which constitutes
something akin to the outside of the inside of the concept and
partakes in the order of the non-discursive, auto-enunciation of

[12] On this Deleuzian reading of 'common notions', see Michael Hardt's fine
commentary 'L'art de l'organisation: agencements ontologiques et agencements
politiques chez Spinoza', *Futur antérieur* 7 (1991). [For a version of this argument in English, see Hardt's *Gilles Deleuze: An Apprenticeship in Philosophy*
(Minneapolis: University of Minnesota Press, 1993), pp. 95–111.]

[13] *Expressionism in Philosophy: Spinoza*, p. 300/322.

[14] [Alliez's recent work, whether in contemporary philosophy, history of philosophy or aesthetics, has been devoted to elucidating the consequences of
affirming the equation Expression = Construction. This is the object in particular of his forthcoming writings on modern painting, with particular reference
to Matisse and Fauvism. See Éric Alliez and Jean-Claude Bonne, *La Pensée-
Matisse* (Paris: Le Passage, 2004) and Éric Alliez and Jean-Clet Martin, *L'Oeil-
cerveau. Histoires de la peinture moderne* (Paris: Le Passage, 2005).]

the event, that which *cannot be defined* because it relates to a nature that is at once more primitive and more complex than 'any assignable surface or volume', to philosophize, to *do* philosophy, is to understand '*why* there are always many infinite movements caught within each other, each folded in the others, *to the extent* [*dans la mesure*] that the return of one instantaneously relaunches another *in such a way* that the plane of immanence is ceaselessly being woven, like a gigantic shuttle' (41/38, my emphasis): Opera-Machine.

To confuse this kind of statement with a simply nominal 'definition' would be especially regrettable. On the contrary, it is the singularizing presupposition of the plane of immanence – as the absolute dimension wherein the ontological fold celebrated by philosophy is exercised – *that guarantees the real character of pseudo-definitions*: pseudo-definitions of the plane of immanence, which does not pre-exist philosophy in order to 'explicate' it, but 'implicates' it as the intuition of the envelopment of the infinite movements of thought, acting like a sieve cast onto chaos, in its mental as much as its physical existence; pseudo-definition of concepts that effectuate intensive sections [*coupes*] of these movements and trace them 'as movements, which are themselves finite, forming, at infinite speed, variable *contours* inscribed on the plane' (45/42). By operating a section of chaos, the plane of immanence calls on concepts, but these concepts in turn *cannot be deduced* from the absolute directions of the plane. As we have seen, the creation of concepts, like the tracing of the plane, is the work of the conceptual persona, through which speculation becomes *ethos* . . . *Personalized* traits of the conceptual persona, *diagrammatic* features of the plane of immanence, *intensive* traits of the concept – these are the three categories, the three modulators (insistence, transistence, consistency) on which philosophical expression depends; or, philosophy as the expression of a constructivism that would be mere protocol or procedure were it not for the Event that exceeds it, and which, in a manner that is not immediately discursive, announces the concept in the processual immanence of its self-positing.

We touch here upon the first significant difference between the philosophical enunciation of concepts and the scientific exposition that resorts to propositions. In effect, 'all [scientific] enunciation is positional [. . .] it remains external to the proposition because the latter's object is a state of affairs as referent [. . .]. On the other hand, [philosophical] positional enunciation is strictly immanent to the concept' (25/23). One will recognize here a possible key to Spinoza's anti-Cartesianism, as developed in his theory of distinctions. Deleuze sums up the question as follows: 'that real distinction is not and cannot be numerical appears to me to be one of the principal themes of the *Ethics*.'[15] This can easily be grasped in terms of the internal logic of Spinozism: God can be said to be cause of all things *in the same sense* that he is said to be cause of himself *if and only if* the unity of substance is not divided by the plurality of attributes, such that the same thing, *formaliter*, constitutes the essence of substance and contains the modal essences. *But how can one express the difference in being without importing real distinction into the absolute?* This problem is no longer in the least Cartesian. It is therefore all the more effective in leading Spinoza to confront Descartes on the grounds of the real distinction, which is necessarily accompanied, according to Descartes, by a substantial division in nature and in things. Indeed, how could God, without turning into an Evil Demon, create things in a way other than the one in which he has given us a clear and distinct idea of them? That is why, as Deleuze explains, Descartes will preserve the traditional distinction between real (numerical) distinction and the (ideal) distinction of reason, whereas Spinoza will rediscover the virtues of the Scotist idea of formal distinction. Formal distinction short-circuits the rule-bound opposition between the first two types of distinction (numerical and ideal), thereby renewing the concept of univocity.

The theory of *distinctio formalis ex natura rei*, whose beauty is matched only by its difficulty, intervenes at this point. It was first introduced by Duns Scotus to explain how divine simplicity is in no way made plural by the trinity of 'persons'. Insofar as the formal distinction of persons does not militate against the reality

---

[15] *Expressionism in Philosophy: Spinoza*, p. 31/38. For what follows, see Part One of the book.

of their common nature, the same principle can be used to think the distinction of the attributes in the unique essence of God. The same applies with Spinoza, since the distinction of divine attributes, univocally predicated of the divine essence, requires that their formal reasons be distinctly present in that same essence, whose unity it is absolutely imperative to preserve. But if formal distinction, according to its most generic formulation, concerns the apprehension of distinct quiddities pertaining to a single subject, there still remains the question of knowing what marks out the *reality* of that distinction. The distinction is real inasmuch as it expresses the effective composition of the multiple forms that constitute the existential unity of a being, and so it will necessarily possess a minimum of real distinction (*minima in suo ordine*) because the really distinct quiddities compose a unique being. Therefore one can say either that the formal distinction refers to an act of understanding that objectively apprehends actually distinct (and hence *de jure* separable) forms without their necessarily being separated (*ratio essendi*); or one can say that for each formally considered notion there is a corresponding being (*ratio cognoscendi*). According to the Scotist formula, *omni entitati formali correspondet adaequate aliquod ens.*[16] In other words, if formal distinction, like all real distinction, precedes the intellect then, unlike real distinction, it is a distinction *secundum quid* – in accordance with a certain point of view that could not precede the possibility of thinking 'formalities' as truly distinct. That is why, *pace* Scotus (for whom *ex natura rei* must be read as *extra intellectum*, 'without any operation of the intellect'), the real is no longer entirely 'separable'

---

[16] Duns Scotus, *Reportata parisiensia 1*, d. 12, q. 2, n. 6. For a fuller analysis of this formula, please see my *Capital Times 1: Tales from the Conquest of Time*, pp. 204–12. Besides the references given there, see Alan B. Wolter, *The Transcendentals and Their Function in the Metaphysics of Duns Scotus* (St. Bonaventure, NY: Franciscan Institute, 1946); and 'The Formal Distinction', in John K. Ryan and Bernardine M. Bonansea (eds.), *John Duns Scotus, 1265–1965* (Washington, DC: Catholic University of America Press, 1965), pp. 52–3; above all, see Ludger Honnefelder, *Ens in quantum ens. Der Begriff des Seienden als solchen als Gegenstand der Metaphysik nach der Lehre des Johannes Duns Scotus*, 2nd ed. (Munster, 1989). [Alliez has thoroughly reappraised the question of Scotism in his *Les Temps capitaux 2/1, L'état de choses* (Paris: Cerf, 1999).]

from the logically possible and the non-contradictorily conceivable. Moreover, divine power is strictly subject to the latter in the affirmation of its own absoluteness.[17]

Descartes – his objections to, and reservations about, Scotist formalism notwithstanding (does it not lead to blasphemy?[18]) – is swept up by this movement of displacement, a movement that inaugurates the path of modern metaphysics by replacing the natural order of the properties of things with a logical order of *a priori* mathematical relations. Once it is sufficient that I am able clearly and distinctly to conceive one thing apart from another, in order to be certain that the one is different from the other, seeing they may at least be made to exist separately, by the omnipotence of God,[19] knowledge is no longer defined in terms of things, according to the in-formation of the intellect by the thing *in genere intelligibili*, but rather on the basis of the concept as objective representation. So it was really with Duns Scotus that the modern translation of *objectum* as 'object' came to be negotiated. Until that point, the *esse objectum* of the thing was only taken to denote its existence (as a being of reason) for the understanding, and not a (formally) distinct entity referring to the *ens qua ens* as the first object of our mind [*entendement*], the transcendental unity common to all genera. Metaphysics, soon to be called *metaphysica generalis*, here turns into the science of the first being [*étant*] *for us*, the transcendental science of a being whose unity of sense is affirmed in the name of a concept so fundamental that soon thereafter it will determine all speculation concerning God as a *metaphysica specialis* (as we can read in the *Opus metaphysicum* of Christoph Scheibler – the 'German Suarez' – Giessen, 1617).

[17] It must be emphasized here that the divine nature is not thereby limited, since contradiction is not an effective possibility. Nevertheless, it remains the case that, in order to define the possible, non-contradiction forces itself upon God to the same extent that it forces itself upon man: *objectively*.

[18] See his letter to Mersenne, dated 6 May 1630: 'And if people understood properly the meaning of their words, they could never say without blasphemy that the truth of something precedes the knowledge that God has of it, for in God willing and knowledge are but one.' *René Descartes: Philosophical Essays and Correspondence*, ed. Roger Ariew, trans. Marjorie Grene and Roger Ariew (Indianapolis: Hackett, 2000), p. 29.

[19] Descartes, *Sixth Metaphysical Meditation*, Adam Tannery edition, vol. IX, p. 62.

What matters here, as far as we're concerned, is perceiving one of the possible readings of the Spinozist rediscovery of the formal distinction. By establishing that which will lead to the scientific ideal of a deductive form of knowledge – starting from the *a priori* analysis of 'clear and distinct' concepts formed by the understanding – the Scotist distinction stands in an unprecedented genealogical relation to the two other distinctions it displaces, in accordance with the principle of a reduction of the real entity [*étant*] to its concept. Enunciated from a position that is strictly immanent to the concept, metaphysical reality passes from the entity to the concept understood as the logical possibility of its object. At first sight, it is *this* immanence that Spinoza intends to expand, by identifying the formal distinction with *all* real distinction (and no longer just its 'minimal' form). But *in fact*, the critique of the Cartesian clear-and-distinct – which targets the logical identification and nominal definition of a concept defined as a being of reason, rather than true knowledge contained in real definitions[20] – leads Spinoza to give an entirely new meaning to the notion of immanence. Immanence will no longer be limited to *reflecting* univocal being as indifferent and neutralized in an abstract concept, that of common nature (*natura communis*), obtained by subtraction from the concrete conditions of existence and by privative indetermination – an abstract concept that had shielded the Subtle Doctor from the accusation of pantheism. Quite the opposite, immanence is now expressed as 'perfectly determinate, as what is predicated in one and the same sense of substance in itself and of modes that are in something else'.[21] 'Univocal being merges with unique, universal and infinite substance: it is posited as *Deus sive natura* [. . .]. With Spinoza, univocal being ceases to be neutralized and become expressive; it becomes a truly expressive and affirmative proposition.'[22] Making knowledge into a kind of expression, and turning the concept itself into a subject, Spinoza proceeds 'in the least abstract fashion possible', that is from 'the source and

[20] They are obliged to express the causal dynamic of production of, in and within [*de/dans*] being.
[21] *Expressionism in Philosophy: Spinoza*, p. 58/67.
[22] *Difference and Repetition*, pp. 58–9/40 [translation modified].

origin of the whole of Nature', of the most concrete possible Nature.[23]

We have incontrovertibly left the territory of an epistemological proposition destined to ensure *a priori* the correlation between thought and being in accordance with the logical ideal of mathematical thinking (what André de Muralt calls the *epistemological expression of the ontological argument*[24]). Instead we are thrown back onto the positivity of an ontological revolution which marks the passage from the indifference of *natura communis* to the pure differentiating power of *natura naturans*. Reduced to his most decisive gesture, Spinoza frees immanence from all its limits, in the naturing self-positing of the movement of the infinite; the actual infinite [*l'infini en acte*], the actual existence of the infinite of, in and within [*de/dans*] nature. The in-finite is the exclusive *preposition* of being, and includes the finite as a mode. This explains why the real distinction is never numerical; conversely, the numerical distinction is never substantial but merely modal, *since all real distinction is formal distinction*. Whence the reversal of the Scotist position according to which the Infinite must primarily belong to the concept of God in order to guarantee the absolute individuality of the divine haecceity, i.e. *before* any distinction of formalities played out within univocal being. The reason for this reversal is that we are now dealing with 'being which is unique, in fact, infinite, that is to say total being beyond which there is nothing'.[25]

---

[23] Spinoza, *Treatise on the Emendation of the Intellect*, § 42, in *The Collected Works of Spinoza*, vol. I, ed. and trans. Edwin Curley (Princeton, NJ: Princeton University Press, 1985), p. 20.

[24] André de Muralt, *L'enjeu de la philosophie medievale. Etudes thomistes, scotistes, occamistes, et gregoriennes* (Leiden: E. J. Brill, 1991), p. 28. However, we do not follow the author's 'classical' interpretation of Spinoza.

[25] Spinoza, *Treatise on the Emendation of the Intellect*, § 42. See the commentary by J.-M. Lespade in 'Substance et infini chez Spinoza', *Revue de Métaphysique et de Morale* 3 (1991), p. 328, note 29, which repeats Deleuze on this point: '. . . for Spinoza the infinite is the mark of a perfect immanence, whilst for Duns Scotus it is the sign of a perfect transcendence'. Nevertheless, in Scotus himself, transcendence experiences a logical fate which only escaped its adversaries via some of his *formalizantes* disciples, beginning with their master Jean de Ripa. (This can be read between the lines of the contrary demonstration by Pierre Vignaux, in 'Être et infini selon Duns Scot et Jean de Ripa' and 'Infini, liberté et histoire du salut', *Studia scolastico-scotistica* (4–5); reprinted in *De Saint Anselme à Luther* [Paris: Vrin, 1976].)

Spinoza, or the infinite becoming-philosophical, 'ascending' [*remonté*] to the event (*Ethics*, Books I and II) and gauging the material practices of its expression (Books III and IV) before finally investing the plane of immanence as the condition of the real experience of becoming (Book V); Spinoza, who made the critique of substantial forms and the conceptual incorporation of an absolutely material becoming into the very expression of philosophy. *Philosophia sive natura*, which is the opposite of a *philosophia perennis*; it conditions the real becoming of thought, its effective work which touches on the 'nature of things' (*rerum natura*): a world-philosophy.

Spinoza, or the 'savage anomaly', according to the forceful expression of Antonio Negri, who was not simply content with hitting on a particularly felicitous title. It is Negri's great merit to have found a way to think together the Spinozist anomaly and the Dutch anomaly and to reveal the latter as what makes the Spinozist position possible; as Deleuze sums up: 'against the Orange family, which represented a *potestas* conforming to the standards of monarchic Europe, the Holland of the De Witt brothers attempted to promote a market conceived as the spontaneity of productive forces or a capitalism conceived as immediate form of the socialisation of forces.'[26] Guaranteeing a maximal expansion of substance and its modes (pantheism *versus* materialism, with the conception of matter as an attribute of God – *sive Deus est res extensa*), and superseding the creationist (or theological) perspective that neutralized univocity in Scotus, the philosophy of Spinoza shows itself to be exemplary in indicating the manner in which 'absolute deterritorialisation on the plane of immanence takes over from a relative deterritorialisation in a given field' (85/88). In fact, insofar as the relative deterritorialization is itself

[26] Gilles Deleuze, preface to the French translation of Antonio Negri's *The Savage Anomaly*, *L'anomalie sauvage* (Paris: PUF, 1982), reprinted in *Deux regimes de fous. Textes et entretiens 1975–1995* (Paris: Minuit, 2003), pp. 175–8. See also Pierre Macherey's excellent presentation of Negri's work, 'Negri: de la médiation à la constitution (description d'un parcours spéculatif)', in *Cahiers Spinoza* 4 (1983), reprinted in his *Avec Spinoza. Études sur la doctrine et l'histoire du spinozisme* (Paris: PUF, 1992). [It is worth noting that Alliez's first published article was a review of Negri's book: 'Spinoza au-delà de Marx', *Critique* 411–12 (1981).]

both horizontal and immanent, '*it combines* with the absolute deterritorialisation of the plane of immanence that carries the movements of relative deterritorialisation to infinity, pushes them to the absolute, by transforming them' (86/90, my emphasis). To put it in yet another way, 'philosophy takes the relative deterritorialisation of capital to the absolute; it makes it pass over onto the plane of immanence as movement of the infinite and suppresses it as internal limit, *turns it back against itself so as to summon forth a new earth, a new people*' (95/99).

It is not the least of the merits of this Marx-inspired analysis that it places the relationship between modern philosophy and capitalism (but the same holds for the relation between ancient philosophy and Athenian imperialism, a different form of immanence: the maritime) under the sign of a *principle of contingent reason*, thereby impugning the validity of the idea of an analytic and necessary reason that would unite 'Western' philosophy with Greece or with Capitalism. The active geography practiced by the authors of *What is Philosophy?* is flatly opposed to all destinal historicisms, whether Hegelian, Husserlian or Heideggerian. Milieus against the origin, geology of the formation of assemblages against genealogy, against the *arkhéologie* of worldviews. That is because self-positing as concept is no longer exercised in the name of a narrative of legitimacy (whether of 'being' or 'the absolute'), but according to the time of a becoming which creates unprecedented assemblages, exceeding history and wresting it from itself, save to fall back into it: 'pure becomings, pure events on a plane of immanence. What History grasps of the event is its effectuation in states of affairs or in lived experience, but the event in its becoming, in its specific consistency, in its self-positing as concept, escapes History' (106/110). Moreover, the concept as becoming is only subject to those forms of affirmation that it determines in its experimentation with what *resists* history and which constitute 'the set of the almost negative conditions' of the event.

That is why the philosophical concept of the concept appears in Deleuze and Guattari in the guise of a pseudo-definition that is *inseparable from a diagnostic operation aimed at our actual becomings*. It is not just Kant, Nietzsche or Foucault who we encounter in this anamorphic projection in which 'the eternal philosophy and the history of philosophy give way to a becoming-philosophical' – *but philosophy tout court*, in the practical singularity of its speculation, as the mirror of a future in which its own history is singularly warped. That is because 'the object of philosophy is not to contemplate the eternal or to reflect history but to diagnose our actual becomings' (107–8/112), becomings that render a *direct* exposition of concepts both possible and necessary. In so doing philosophy turns to the singular point that constitutes it, in the reciprocal relation of the concept and creation and in accordance with a pedagogy of the concept that is also its material ontology. Would Spinoza's materialist imagination still be so crucial today, if it did not pre-emptively trouble the self-confidence of a pretension – that of idealism, as embodied in its threefold universalist avatar: the objective idealism of contemplation, the subjective idealism of reflection and the intersubjective idealism of communication? Opening up thought to constituent power, Spinoza is our contemporary by virtue of his refusal of any dialectical dimension that would aim at the (utopian or historical) reconciliation of the real.[27]

To make philosophy and its history revolve around the Spinozist mystery ('and the greatest philosophers are hardly more than apostles who distance themselves from or draw near to this mystery' [58/60]) is to rescue philosophy from the illusion of a discursiveness that could be grasped in terms of the entrainment of sense within a superior dialectic. Such a discursiveness, having detached the concept from the philosophical problem *specified* with respect to the plane of immanence presupposed by

[27] On this problematic, see Antonio Negri, 'L'antimodernité de Spinoza', in *Spinoza Subversif: Variations (In)actuelles* (Paris: Kimé, 1994), pp. 111–29. This volume brings together a series of articles dedicated to Spinoza that Negri wrote in the period after the publication of *The Savage Anomaly* (and also includes an introduction by Emilia Giancotti). The question of 'antimodernity' or of the *Oltre il moderno* (beyond the modern) is further developed in its own right – *that is to say, politically* – from the Spinozist standpoint of the *ontological power of a multitude of co-operating singularities* in Negri's *Il Potere costituente. Saggio sulle alternative del moderno* (Varèse, Sugarco Edizioni, 1992); trans. Maurizia Boscaglia as *Insurgencies: Constituent Power and the Modern State* (Minneapolis: University of Minnesota, 1999).

the concept, does nothing but link opinions to one other. *Urdoxa*: when the formulas of the world present themselves as the Promethean moments of the concept, Spinoza becomes the Enemy who must be suppressed, *aufgehoben* (Jacobi, Fichte, Hegel elevate Spinoza to the rank of a genuine conceptual persona). We will therefore consider 'the time rather than the history of philosophy [. . .] a grandiose time of coexistence [. . .] the coexistence of planes, not the succession of systems' (58–9/58–9); a stratigraphic rather than a chronological time; a *problematic* time marked by the superimposition of planes of immanence, each referring back to an image of thought as the problem conditioning the creation of its concepts (cases of solution) and the invention of its conceptual personae (events of thought). It is the conceptual personae who 'constitute points of view according to which planes of immanence are distinguished from one another or brought together' (73/75) – keeping in mind however that 'images of thought cannot arise in any order whatever because they involve changes of orientation that can be directly located only on the earlier image' (58/58). That is also how the conceptual persona animates or expresses *the* plane of immanence, the geological coexistence of all the planes it has had to cross in order to maintain its role: *to show thought's territories, its absolute deterritorializations and reterritorializations* (67/69).

To retrace this movement, we must understand that the conceptual persona is the Adventurer and that three propositions may be extracted from its adventures; these propositions carry the natural phenomenology of the conceptual persona's apparition: 1) every territory presupposes a prior deterritorialization which enables the diagnosis of *types*; because 2) the earth is ceaselessly carrying out a deterritorialization 'on the spot' [*sur place*] that *personalizes* the movement of those who leave their territories behind – 'with crayfish that set off walking in file at the bottom of the water, with pilgrims or knights who ride a celestial line of flight' (82/85): the earth becomes indistinguishable from the movement of *its own personae*; 3) deterritorialization becomes absolute when the earth passes onto the pure plane of immanence of a thought and when the persona reveals itself to

be a thinker – or a *conceptual persona*. It is because the genealogy of the persona is inseparable from the material geology of
thought ('the conceptual persona and the plane of immanence
presuppose each other' [73/75]) that we are forced to counte-
nance the idea of a Copernican revolution putting thought in a
direct relationship with the earth: 'Thinking is neither a line
drawn between subject and object nor a revolving of one around
the other. Rather, thinking takes place in the relationship of territory and the earth' (82/85).

From this perspective, we must begin to articulate the fact that
ever since the *Anti-Oedipus* Deleuze and Guattari never ceased
affirming an 'ecosophic' becoming of philosophy, another way of
conceiving reason and its becomings, countering the 'objectal'
logic that supposedly presides over the 'accomplishment of
Western Metaphysics' as onto-ego-theology. To be more succinct: *onto-ethology contra onto-theology* – Spinoza, always.

We have now reached the point of maximal tension between, on
the one hand, an onto-*teleology* that seeks to deduce, from the
Scotist model of the *ens in quantum ens*, the historial necessity of
an 'object' that has become the exclusive subject of modern
metaphysics (homogenesis), given the identification of the *ens* to
the *res*[28] in the 'mathelogical' conquest of the horizon of representation (that which 'objects itself' [*s'objecte*] *to* a subject, that
which founds every *res* in its reality); on the other, an *onto*-logy
that inscribes its constructivism under the sign of a principle of
contingent reason, a principle on which the plane of immanence
itself must depend (heterogenesis), in order to express absolute
necessity as the constitutive contingency of being 'constructing'
itself – dynamic constitution, imagination realized. According to
this second reading, which consists in 'eventalizing' rather than
historicizing the history of philosophy, Spinoza would be a
mystery rather than a 'reference'. What's more – *and it is precisely
something more* – doesn't his naturalism manifest the affirmative

---

[28] As Suarez puts it: *ens in quantum ens reale esse objectum adaequatum huius
scientiae*. One can, and indeed must, refer to Jean-François Courtine's important book, *Suarez et le système de la métaphysique* (Paris: PUF 1990), for a rigorous analysis of this unique proposition.

irruption of affective contingency and phenomenality ('we do not know what a body can do . . .') on a plan(e) that had thereto tended to subordinate the univocity of being to the methodical optic of the *ratio abstractissima entis*? (*Mathematica haec est ontologikè*: it is by way of this phrase that Rodolphus Goclenius 'quite conceivably [. . .] forged the word ontology for the first time'.[29]) But ontology will neither be named nor summoned under the strictly epistemological heading of mathematical abstraction without arousing its power to produce afresh, in and by concepts that express themselves in the world – naturalism as philosophy.

Under the sign of modernity we would thus be witness to something like a double birth of ontology. In the first birth, the plan(e) defines itself according to universals – or transcendentals: what supersedes (*transcendere*) the entity [*l'étant*] *qua* singular – whose power [*pouvoir*] depends on the neutralization of being in an abstract concept (instigator and tributary of a *mathesis universalis*) 'objected' [*s'objectant*] to the subject which it institutes in its certainty as *ego*. In the second birth, the plane of immanence is nothing other than this power [*puissance*], abstract but perfectly real, common to all beings (souls, bodies, non-

---

[29] Courtine, pp. 408–13, especially p. 410. See also, by the same author, the entry 'Res' in the *Historisches Wörterbuch der Philosophie*, ed. Joachim Ritter and Karlfried Grunder (Stuttgart/Basel: Schwabe, 1971–1991). In this article, Courtine reminds us that Avicennian 'formal ontology' – in which *res* is defined by the *certitudo qua et id quod ist*, a certainty that guarantees it its own being, which is not that of an existent but of a *quidditas* – provides the framework on the basis of which Arab algebra will introduce, in the role of unknown variable, the 'thing' (*al saya', res ignota*), 'whilst Italian mathematics formulated in the vernacular witnesses in the following centuries the appearance of the word *cosa*'. Let us note that the term 'ontology' is also present in the *Theatrum philosophicum* by Jacobus Lohardus, published in the same year (1613) as Goclenius's *Lexicon philosophicum*. [Very recent research by Raul Corazzon, basing himself on Wilhelm Risse's *Bibliographia philosophica vetus* (New York: Georg Olms, 1998), points towards a precedence of Lohardus in this regard, as testified by the title of his 1606 work, published in St. Gallen, *Ogdoas Scholastica continens Diagraphen Typicam atrium: Grammatices (Latina, Graeca), Logices, Rhetorices, Astronomices, Ethices, Physices, Metaphysices, seu Ontologia*. Only two copies of this book are reputed to be in existence, they are held at the Staatsbibliothek Augsburg and the Lüneburg Ratsbibliothek. See www.formalontology.it/history.htm.]

formed elements) that singularize themselves on this modal plane according to their *affects* – affects by virtue of which each 'thing', in acting, living, striving to preserve its own being ('three ways of saying the same thing'[30]) is 'nothing but the actual essence of the thing',[31] such that each 'thing' ends up affecting the whole of nature and instituting being as an object of pure affirmation immanent to modes of existence in Habit.[32] In other words, we are dealing here with the *practice of singular essence* as an individuating force constitutive of the organization of the body and the affinity of souls (*ethica*). Here 'there is no longer a subject, but only individuating affective states of an anonymous force. The plane is concerned only with movements and rests, with dynamic affective charges: the plane will be perceived with whatever it makes us perceive, and then only bit by bit. Our ways of living, thinking or writing change according to the plane upon which we find ourselves'.[33]

This means that here *Mind does not know itself, except insofar as it perceives the ideas of the affections of the Body*.[34] Furthermore, there will be as many species and degrees of soul as there are species and degrees of composition of life, in accordance with the principle of an infinite 'animation' whose first effect will be to transform the objective genitive – the idea of a body – into a subjective genitive – the thought *of* this body – *extending* to all concrete individualities, all the way to the simplest of bodies. Following a scale of differential complexity which allows us to ascend to the Infinite, 'we conceive that the whole of nature is a single Individual whose parts, that is, all bodies, vary in an infinity of ways without

---

[30] Spinoza, *Ethics*, Book IV, Proposition 24, in *The Collected Works of Spinoza*, vol. I, ed. and trans. Edwin Curley (Princeton, NJ: Princeton University Press, 1985).

[31] *Ethics*, IIIP7.

[32] See Laurent Bove, 'L'habitude, activité fondatrice de l'existence actuelle dans la philosophie de Spinoza', in *Revue philosophique de la France et l'étranger*, January–March 1991, especially p. 46, where he identifies the 'ontogenetic' horizon of Habit as *the very constitution of the organization of bodies*.

[33] *Spinoza: Practical Philosophy*, pp. 172–3/128 [translation modified].

[34] *Ethics* IIP23 (my emphasis). This is a decisive consequence of Proposition 13, according to which '[T]he object of the idea constituting the human Mind is the Body, or a certain mode of Extension which actually exists, and nothing else.'

changing the whole Individual'.[35] This Individual is the source of 'an infinite power [*potentia*] of thinking which, insofar as it is infinite, contains within itself the whole of Nature ideally, and whose thoughts proceed in the same manner as does Nature, which is in fact the object of its thought'.[36] Essence – which is constitutive of all that is, since it is no longer determined *a priori* by a generic or specific notion whose identity would serve as the basis of the individual – is that power of self-affirmation whereby all individuation is defined in the real movement of its linkages with the world (from the Idea as act to essence as productivity). This means that individuality becomes indistinguishable from the constitutive dynamic of being, which composes the totality of things and itself forms an Individual whose infinite power of thought will be given in Nature for the same reason and on the same plane as the *facies totius universi* according to the order of extension . . . And thus 'the order and connection of ideas is the same as the order and connection of things and, vice versa, the order and connection of things is the same as the order and connection of ideas'.[37]

As a Spinozist, you will define the philosopher by the affects and events he has been able to snatch from chaos in the process of

[35] *Ethics*, IIL7, Scholium. Putting all theology aside, 'bodies are distinguished from one another by reason of motion and rest, speed and slowness, and not by reason of substance' (II L1), which I read along with IIIP57 Scholium. On these questions, see Hans Jonas's essay 'Spinoza and the Theory of Organism', in *Philosophical Essays: From Ancient Creed to Technological Man* (Chicago: University of Chicago Press, 1974), in particular pp. 218–23; the title of the essay hints, albeit obliquely, at the Whiteheadian development of this 'animist' theme under the rubric of a philosophy of the organism, and at a second universal ontology – Spinoza's *Ethics* being the 'first universal ontology', according to Husserl, who nevertheless makes clear that: 'It is a complete misunderstanding to interpret Spinoza according to what is visible on the surface of his "geometrical" method of demonstration.' See *The Crisis of European Sciences and Transcendental Phenomenology*, trans. David Carr (Evanston, IL: Northwestern University Press, 1970), p. 64.

[36] Spinoza, *Letter XXXII* to Oldenberg, 20 November 1665.

[37] *Ethics* VP1, Dem. Brunschvicg concludes, in a quasi-Deleuzian tone, that 'with Spinoza, it is legitimate to say that philosophy ceases to signify a system in the historic succession of like systems, to become something which experiences itself from the inside and justifies itself by the very fact that *it is comprehended*' (*Le progrès de la conscience dans la philosophie occidentale*, vol. I [Paris: Librairie Félix Alcan, 1927], p. 173, my emphasis.)

constructing a plane of immanence capable, through concepts, of conferring an appropriate consistency to the virtual – a virtual which in turn imposes a new cut [*découpage*] on the 'real'. That is why, if there is no principle of philosophical reason save for that of a contingent reason acting prior to [*en deçà*] anything that is presented *a posteriori* as tradition, this contingency testifies to a practical reason with a grip on the untimely becoming of the actual (Spinoza's 'anti-modernity' is exemplary vis-à-vis this question of tradition, launched as it was against a Cartesian modernity that did not come into the world as 'classical'; and to think of the material forces, probable and improbable, which were involved in that confrontation!). Being empiricist, synthetic and ethological (it requires an encounter, a conjunction), this kind of reason is engaged in the study of the powers to affect and to be affected that characterize all things and their becoming, with the aim of extracting the possibility of something being produced afresh. This production is in turn related to that critical point when the stifled forces of the present appeal to 'a new earth, a new people' – that is, to a new composition of forces. The novelty in question is that of a self-positing that lets itself be grasped according to the event's regime of excess (i.e. excess vis-à-vis its historical effectuation in states of affairs). Therefore, we could say that philosophy becomes political in this 'utopian' conjunction of the concept with actuality; or that by pursuing its path of immanence in the transpositional movement of the infinite, *the revolution of the concept encounters the concept of revolution* as the correlate of its creation: a presentation of the infinite in the finitude of the here-and-now.[38] In what is surely one of the book's most beautiful passages, that is what Deleuze and Guattari call 'the constitutive relationship of philosophy with non-philosophy'. And again, in a formula that encapsulates the very sense of their work: 'the philosopher must become non-philosopher so that non-philosophy becomes the earth and people of philosophy' (105/109).

Philosophy thus becomes the concern of a becoming-philosophy that treats the plane of immanence as a field of radical

[38] [The original discussion of the concepts glossed here is in *What is Philosophy?* pp. 95–7/99 101.]

experience and experimentation. To make becoming into the concept itself, the concept we do not have, the concept we must forge for ourselves in nomadism, in becoming philosophers and non-philosophers, and something else besides.[39] Turning the concept into a singularity, like a habit contracted contemplating the elements from whence we emerged . . . This programme has never stopped haunting the modernity of those who paid for the concept (which they have but are not [*qu'ils ont et ne sont pas*]) with the loss of the plane of immanence, and who must, as a result, reterritorialize themselves on consciousness (the ground rent of the French), or use the latter as a means of deterritorialization (the Germans' infinite quest). 'England, from this point of view, is Germany's obsession, for the English are precisely those nomads' for whom there is no subject other than practice,

---

[39] A confrontation with the Fichtean standpoint would be of particular interest here, since the investment of reflection as the faculty of concepts *in general*, 'the state of mind [*Zustand der Gemuts*] in which we first prepare ourselves to find out the subjective conditions under which we can arrive at concepts' (Immanuel Kant, *Critique of Pure Reason*, trans. Paul Guyer and Allen W. Wood [Cambridge: Cambridge University Press, 1998], A 260–B316, p. 366), leads Fichte to renounce the 'guiding thread' of logic and to confront the question of the *thinking* dimension of thought 'on the basis of non-knowledge'. The vital affinity between philosophical and artistic intuition is here *as clear as day*, to paraphrase Fichte's *Sonneklarer Bericht* of 1801. (For 'the *whole* virtuality of sensible intuition is contained in the activity of thought', Martial Guéroult, *L'Évolution et la structure de la Doctrine de la science chez Fichte*, vol. 1 [Paris, 1930], p. 180.) But the following is no less clear: Fichtean gnosogony must take on a *systematic* character in order to reveal the knowledge of knowledge in its unconditioned form as absolute knowledge; the passage through non-philosophy serves as a pedagogy of the foundation, in its exteriority to the founded, the illustration (*Abbildung*) of the originary indistinction between concept and intuition in the *pure Ego* [*Ich*] which reflects the not-being-conceivable (*Unbegreiflichkeit*) of the absolute. Whence the fact that 'our philosophical thought signifies nothing and does not possess the least content: only the thought *thought* in this thinking possesses a signification and a content' (*Ruckerinnerungen* . . ., in *Sämmtliche Werke*, V, p. 341). Between *Urwhares* (1803) and *Urbild* (1813), the *Science of Knowledge* of 1804 accepts the rights of this 'necessity' by asserting itself as a realism that subordinates Knowledge to the Absolute – to the reality of an absolute originary Ego – which is manifested within it. On the continuity between Fichte's first and second philosophy, and the anachronistic character of the interpretation of the absolute Ego as transcendental illusion proposed by Reinhard Lauth and especially Alexis Philonenko, see Robert Lamblin, 'Sur la nouvelle interprétation de la philosophie de Fichte', *Les Études philosophiques*, January–March 1989, pp. 86–90.

no way of living and thinking other than inhabiting. 'For them a tent is all that is needed' to upset the sedentary distribution of categories and impose their own *erewhon* landscape (101/105). A 'tent' is precisely a complex of space and time that could never serve as the object of any recognition whatsoever.

Like a distant echo of the three moments of the univocity of being – Duns Scotus, Spinoza, Nietzsche – expounded in *Difference and Repetition*,[40] it should be up to a Nietzschean-inspired reason to inaugurate the play of *geo-philosophical difference*.[41]

[40] See pp. 57–60/39–41 and 387–8/303–4. And let's not forget the following lapidary formula: 'Philosophy merges with ontology, but ontology merges with the univocity of being', *Logique du sens* (Paris: Minuit, 1969), p. 210; *The Logic of Sense,* ed. Constantin V. Boundas, trans. Mark Lester with Charles J. Stivale (London: Athlone Press, 1990), p. 179.

[41] It is incontestably under this 'geophilosophical' rubric that Jean-Pierre Faye deploys his 'narrative reason'. See *La Raison narrative* (Paris: Balland, 1990).

II The Aetiology of Science

The first cosmonaut is the hermeneut.

Alain de Libera

Given the textual economy of *What is Philosophy?* (Part II – 'Philosophy, Science, Logic and Art'), the question regarding the status of the *necessity* by which the geo-philosophical principle of contingency must oppose itself to the time of science and the 'series' of scientific progress, both of which are covered by the regime of *necessary reason*, remains in abeyance. Under the guise of a quest for real distinction, does this double necessity not reintroduce a transcendent point of view that would lead philosophy to judge 'scientific understanding' in the name of a 'speculative reason' – an alternative reason, to be sure, but one that in the end might still retain no less of a determining position vis-à-vis the very concept of science? Such a predicament would be especially deplorable, since in this unequal chiasmus self-positing would acquire a dialectical position of identity, determining its outside as a moment of its own negativity. Hegel's posthumous revenge on Spinoza, perhaps? We could of course challenge the coherence of this line of questioning in the name of the very letter of the text. If our two authors, without the least hesitation, relate 'their' self-positing of the concept to its self-movement in Hegel (for whom the Absolute never possesses a referential value), it is only immediately to remark that 'an indeterminate extension of philosophy [. . .] left scarcely any

independent movement of the arts and sciences remaining'
(16/12).[1] Keeping in mind Foucault's warning about the difficulty
of really escaping from the clutches of Hegel, let us press on.[2]
Stated as it is from a philosophical standpoint, does the estab-

[1] In spite of his declared anti-Hegelianism (see for example his
'Mathématique et philosophie', *Les Cahiers de Paris VIII*, 1991; translated as
'Philosophy and Mathematics: Infinity and the End of Romanticism' in
Theoretical Writings, ed. and trans. Ray Brassier and Alberto Toscano [London:
Continuum, 2004]), Alain Badiou's philosophy is not exempt from a similar criti-
cism: one could say that it rekindles the destiny of 'an old conception of the
higher philosophy' (144/152), which leads the unconditioned concept to find the
totality of its generic conditions in the functions it dominates. To follow this
thought to its conclusion: in the name of a mathematical ontology, this destiny
applies equally to 'Platonism' and to 'Lacanianism'. For further analysis of the
'ecclesial' nature of this 'post-Lacanian Platonism which mathematises the
event and names the unnameable', see Jacques Rancière's essay in *Cahiers du
Collège International de philosophie* 8 (1989), pp. 211–15. Pierre Verstraeten has
proposed a provocative reading of Badiou's *L'Être et l'événement* by analysing
the 'convergence of fidelities' between Badiou and Heidegger, see 'Philosophies
de l'événement: Badiou et quelques autres', *Les Temps modernes* 529–530
(1990), pp. 241–61. Finally, let us note that it is on the occasion of a 'contrast-
ing re-exposition of the thought of Deleuze' that Badiou offers in 'five punctu-
ations' the best exposition of his own most recent philosophy ('Gilles Deleuze,
The Fold: Leibniz and the Baroque', trans. Thelma Sowley, in *Gilles Deleuze and
the Theater of Philosophy*, ed. Constantin V. Boundas and Dorothea Olkowski
[London: Routledge, 1994] pp. 51–69). The exercise is repeated by François
Wahl in his preface to Badiou's *Conditions*, entitled 'Le soustractif' (Paris: Seuil,
1992), pp. 10–29. In *De l'impossibilité de la phénoménologie. Sur la philosophie
française contemporaine* (Paris: Vrin, 1995), I showed that a philosophical field
*with a grip on the present – in other words, contemporary philosophy as an ontol-
ogy of the present* – could be and must be thought starting from the idea of a
maximal ontological tension between Deleuze and Badiou. In my view, Deleuze
and Badiou constitute the extreme polarities of the contemporary field, such as
the latter divergently [*à contresens*] articulates its materialist necessity into singularities and multiplicities. See, in the wake of the publication of Badiou's
Deleuze in 1997, my articles in *Futur Antérieur* 43 (1997–1998), *Multitudes* 1
(2000) and 6 (2001) and, most recently, '*Anti-Oedipus*: Thirty Years On', trans.
Alberto Toscano, *Radical Philosophy* 124 (2004), pp. 6–12.
[2] Michel Foucault, *L'ordre du discours* (Paris: Gallimard, 1971), pp. 74–5;
trans. Rupert Swyer as 'The Discourse on Language', in *The Archaeology of
Knowledge* (New York: Pantheon Books, 1972), p. 235: 'But truly to escape
Hegel involves an exact appreciation of the price we have to pay to detach ourselves from him. It assumes that we are aware of the exact extent to which Hegel,
insidiously perhaps, is close to us; it implies a knowledge, in that which permits
us to think against Hegel, of that which remains Hegelian. We have to determine
the extent to which our anti-Hegelianism is possibly one of his tricks directed
against us, at the end of which he stands, motionless, waiting for us.'

lishment of the difference between the philosophical concept and the scientific function not oblige us to rely on a hierarchical principle – a principle that is all the more inevitable inasmuch as the question of science necessarily enters as a constituent element into the enunciation of the 'problem of philosophy in relation to the Now rather than to the eternal'? Which is why 'concepts *necessarily* involve allusions to science' (153/162, my emphasis).

The *precision* of the war machine launched by *What is Philosophy?* against so-called analytic philosophy depends largely on the response to this question. When the word 'philosophy' no longer designates anything but the target for the logic of propositions, since 'a real hatred inspires logic's rivalry with, or its will to supplant, philosophy' (133/140). But who would want to deny that rivalries no less pointed exist between science and philosophy? After all, it was Einstein's derision that made Bergson recoil, as he tried to rival for 'precision' with the men of science.

So, what image of science?

On an important point, if I'm not mistaken, the way in which Deleuze and Guattari take up the question of science bears some affinity with Albert Lautman's critical analysis of the relations between physics and mathematics. For our present purposes, it suffices to recall that by fighting on two fronts – against logical empiricism and dogmatic idealism – and by bringing these two fronts together in a single battle against the obliteration of the real, Lautman sought to develop a very different project, one that would make room for an 'intrinsic characterisation of the real', thus setting him apart from any kind of verificationism. As he explains, 'a philosophy of science that would not dedicate itself entirely to the study of the solidarity between domains of reality and methods of investigation would be wholly devoid of interest'.[3]

What is the *interest* of *What is Philosophy?* from the point of view of a philosophy of science *and* of nature, if it does not lie in

[3] Albert Lautman, *Essai sur l'unité des mathématiques et divers écrits* (Paris: UGE, 1977), p. 28 and 281. It is worth bearing in mind the importance that Deleuze accords to Lautman in *Difference and Repetition*.

the attempt to sketch the programme for a physical ontology up to the task of superseding the opposition between 'physicalism' and 'phenomenology' by *integrating* the physico-mathematical phenomenology of scientific thought into a superior materialism founded on a general dynamics? Hence the need to set this 'solidarity' in motion by providing it with an initial content, thereby permitting the formation of the *material concept* of the science which this content identifies itself with. The diversion [*détournement*] of Bergsonian (immediate) intuition is prepared both before *and* beyond [*en deçà et au-delà*] the realism-idealism opposition, *when the act of knowing tends to coincide with the act that generates the real.* As we read in Deleuze-Guattari, 'it is by slowing down that matter, as well as the scientific thought able to penetrate it with propositions, is actualised' (112/118).

What do they mean by 'slowing down'? Let us pause and consider the respective attitudes of science and of philosophy toward chaos. Whilst philosophy must engage the infinite speed of chaos in order to select and extract the infinite movements of the thought that cuts through it – thereby giving consistency to the virtual through concepts (so that the event, a virtual becomes consistent, can then breathe its specific life into the concept) – science relinquishes the infinite in order to produce a reference capable of actualizing the virtual by *functions*. The best formula is the most succinct: if the concept is a section of chaos, 'a function is a Slow-motion'.

Before running through the theses that follow from this stance, let us note immediately that taken together these theses make up a veritable *cosmogenesis*, which associates the opening up of the modern theory of science to the constitution of the world as a determined totality. *Philosophical constructivism makes room for scientific functionalism.* This is a functionalism according to which, far from the limited thing imposing a limit on the infinite (a slowing down), it is 'the limit that makes possible a limited thing' (113/120). Genesis is thus conceived as the introduction of notions relative to the concrete into the heart of an analysis of the limit: a 'proto-genesis'. We thus get the following theses:

1. *Proto-limit*: 'To slow down is to set a limit in chaos to which all speeds are subject, so that they form a variable determined as

abscissa, at the same time as the limit forms a universal constant that cannot be gone beyond [. . .] and reference is [. . .] the relationship of the variable, as abscissa of speeds, with the limit' (112/118–9) which in turn finds itself enveloped in a proto-temporality.

2a. *Framing*: 'When the limit generates an abscissa of speeds by slowing down, the virtual forms of chaos tend to be actualised in accordance with an ordinate' (114/121) . . .

2b. *Thing-function* [*fonction de chose*]: . . . such that 'the limit is now the origin of a system of coordinates [. . .] on which a third variable depends as state of affairs [*état de chose*] or formed matter in the system [. . .] it is a complex variable that depends on a relation between at least two independent variables' (115/121–2).[4]

Consequently, *in a formed physical system the state of affairs* [*état de chose*] *is a function indexed to a linearity of order which is itself marked by an irreversible facticity*.[5]

3. *Potential*: nevertheless, we must avoid turning the function into 'the sovereign power of thought over being, which no absolute boundary can thwart' (Natorp), as the Neo-Kantians wished to do by reducing the given to mere *data* of mathematical analysis in the development of the *a priori*. If in fact the state of affairs functions only as the actuality of an ordered 'mixture' of variables (particle-trajectories, signs-speeds . . .), 'a state of affairs [*état de chose*] does not actualise a chaotic virtual without taking from it a *potential* that is distributed in the system of coordinates. From the virtual that it actualises it draws a potential that it appropriates' (116/122), without which it would be devoid of activity, starting with the 'cascade of actualisations' that lets us pass from the state of affairs to the referable thing, and from the thing to the individuated body.

4. *Problem*: potential is the *problem* of function insofar as it creates singularities and 'all kinds of bifurcations on a plane of reference that does not preexist its detours or its layout' (117/123). Potential is the problem *of* the sense of physics in its

---

[4] [Translation modified.]
[5] On this question of physical systems, see Lautman, pp. 146–7.

difference from the sense of mathematics, to the extent that it is no longer 'simply' a case of providing initial conditions but rather of referring to a Giver [*un Donnant*]. Potential is thus a reminder to mathematics that every quantitative description is by its very nature approximate and that the constraints of physics do not lead towards a degradation of mathematical rigour, but rather to the invention of a new *physico-mathematical* rigour which had thereto been covered up by classical determinist idealization.[6] It is through potential that the state of affairs 'can confront accidents, adjunctions, ablations or even projections, as we see in geometrical figures: either losing and gaining variables, extending singularities up to the neighbourhood of new ones, or following bifurcations that transform it [. . .] or, above all, individuating bodies in the field that it forms with the potential. None of these operations come about all by themselves; they all constitute "problems"' (145/153–4).

Appropriating what differs in kind from any supposedly *preexisting* proposition, science *in the making* forbids itself the deduction of a unification of the Referent that would result in the establishment of a logistics incapable of regulating experimentation and confronting the question of matter (we do not know what matter can do . . .). This does not bring the function closer to the concept, but rather serves to confirm the difference between them, since states of affairs retain from virtual events only the 'potentials already in the course of being actualised, forming part of the functions' (152/160). That these states of affairs are projected 'into necessarily orientated systems of reference' (118/125) points to *the actuality of the capture of potential*.

---

[6] On this subject, we would ideally need to cite practically everything written by Ilya Prigogine and Isabelle Stengers from *La Nouvelle Alliance* onwards. But in particular, we would like to draw the reader's attention to Appendix I in the new edition (Paris: Gallimard, 1986) and to 'La querelle du déterminisme, six ans après', in *La querelle du déterminisme* (Paris: Gallimard, 1990), especially pp. 254–5. [The English translation of *La Nouvelle Alliance*, *Order out of Chaos*, differs substantially from the original French, the most notable difference being the omission of the extended and sympathetic discussions of contemporary French philosophy of science in general, and Deleuze in particular, which feature in the original.]

5. *Partial Observer*: we find the same movement interiorized at the level of the respective subjects of enunciation of philosophy and science. The partial observer is here juxtaposed to the conceptual persona. The observer is partial because 'there is no total observer that, like Laplace's "demon", is able to calculate the future and the past starting from a given state of affairs' (122/129). Here we must stress that in order to be fully achieved the rupture with the ideal of intelligibility belonging to classical dynamics demands that the partiality of observers manifest something other than a limit of knowledge or the role of subjectivity within scientific enunciation.[7] As it happens, it is precisely the constitution of science on the basis of a function, finding its origin in the limit *qua* slowing down, that gives its properly intrinsic signification to relativism. In fact, far from being relative to a subject, relativism 'constitutes not a relativity of truth but, on the contrary, a truth of the relative, that is to say, of variables whose cases it orders according to the values it extracts from them in its system of coordinates' (123/130). The partial observer expresses the ideal point of view that lets one both perceive and test the sensible forces integrated in the functions. Situated in the neighbourhood of singularities, these perceptions and affections belong to the functives themselves ('even geometric figures have affections and perceptions' . . .) as well as to the things studied ('even when they are nonliving, or rather inorganic, things have a lived experience because they are perceptions and affections' [146/154]). Now transposed to the level of partial observers, we re-encounter the Deleuzian theme of a *superior empiricism* dedicated to the transgression of the supreme principle of Kantianism – with its axis set in the 'possibility' of experience – in the direction of the discovery of spatio-temporal dynamics irreducible to the notion of a 'schematism'. The partial observer becomes the scientific name for force, inasmuch as force does nothing but 'perceive and experience' – 'as Leibniz and Nietzsche knew' (124/130) – that is, inasmuch as force can qualify a state of affairs as a process.

---

[7] On the 'quantum' actualization of this question, see Ilya Prigogine and Isabelle Stengers, *Entre le temps et l'éternité* (Paris: Fayard, 1988), ch. 6.

At the end of this trajectory, the scientific formula of speculative materialism takes shape [*prend corps*]. *In the real*, or according to 'a characterisation intrinsic to the real' (to borrow Lautman's expression), it identifies the objective phenomenology of the observer – *partial insofar as it is immanent* – with the *force of the sensible*. Against the functional idealism of a *logic of pure knowledge* which rejects the sensible as a principle,[8] Deleuze and Guattari relate the modern concept of science (the function) to the emergence of a physical ontology of manifestation *conditioned* by the experimental moment in which 'affects become energetic relationships, and perception itself becomes a quantity of information' (126/132).

To paraphrase a well-known formula from *Difference and Repetition*, I am tempted to say that the principle of reason deployed by the function is *strangely bent* [*étrangement coudé*]. On the one hand, it leans towards that which it *necessarily* grounds, and this is science's 'trans-descendant'[9] movement of slowing down: from chaotic virtuality to states of affairs and bodies that actualize chaos through the function. On the other hand, it is subjected to the pressure of the virtual through the potential it appropriates; it then attempts to 're-ascend' the infinite contingency that resists the oriented actualization of the *sufficiency* of its principle in order to wrest away a part of the secret haunting science – the secret of the chaos rumbling away behind it. This gives us a better grasp of the importance of 'turbulences' and other 'strange' or chaotic attractors. It also sheds light, retrospectively, on the philosophico-scientific debates around the status of the differential calculus: the origin of mathematical physics is revealed as being *de facto* contemporary with 'the constitution of a chaosmos internal to modern science' (194/206).[10] When the various branches of mathematics take

[8] Hermann Cohen, *Logik der reinen Erkenntnis* (Berlin: B. Cassirer, 1902).

[9] [The expression, together with its converse, 'trans-ascendant', was first coined by the French philosopher Jean Wahl.]

[10] Apart from *What is Philosophy?* (193/205), we could also refer to the now 'classic' analysis provided in Chapter IV of *Difference and Repetition*, as well as to the one in *The Fold: Leibniz and the Baroque*, ch. 2. – The very title of Lagrange's great treatise is the best summary of the object and stakes of this debate: *A Theory of Analytical Functions Containing the Principle of Differential*

variation as their object, it is not without relating variation to the infinite and making it infinite . . . [*sans porter et rapporter la variation à l'infini*]. Everything happens then as if science's struggle with chaos turns *within itself* 'against properly scientific opinion as *Urdoxa*, which consists sometimes in determinist prediction (Laplace's God) and sometimes in probabilistic evaluation (Maxwell's demon): by releasing itself from initial pieces of information and large-scale pieces of information, science substitutes for communication the conditions of creativity defined by singular effects and minimal fluctuations' (194/206–7).

A new alliance *of* the function?[11] This suggests a non-standard functionalism required by a thoroughgoing naturalism (that is, as we shall verify, an *ontologically charged* naturalism).

Apologies to those in a rush, but this massive 'note to the reader' was needed to do justice to the sovereign progression of our argument and allow us finally to confront the question from which we started out. *When everything's in the balance*, what image of science?

We must start again from the question of the establishment of a non-hierarchical and non-hierarchizing difference (between science and philosophy) and consider its importance for the *war economy* of a book that is, in its entirety, set against the reductionist meta-logic that, in the name of building a 'scientific philosophy'* (or of what remains of the analytic doctrine of the *a*

Calculus, Separated from any Consideration of the Infinitely Small, the Vanishing, Limits and Fluxions, and Reduced to the Algebraic Analysis of Finite Quantities (Paris, 1797). On the 'impurity' of the origins of differential calculus, the classic text remains Berkeley's 1734 *The analyst*.

[11] [The reference is to the original title of Prigogine and Stengers's *Order Out of Chaos* – see note 7.]

* (POST-)ANALYTICAL NOTE 2: According to Rudolf Carnap's (in 'The Overcoming of Metaphysics through the Logical Analysis of Language', in A.J. Ayer [ed.], *Logical Positivism* [New York: Macmillan, 1959]), 'scientific philosophy' means: substitution of philosophy with the 'logic of science', i.e. with an *entirely analytical logical syntax*. Reading Carnap, one will agree that, at its origin, 'analytical philosophy' does *not* have 'philosophy' as one of its constituent terms. But in fact, ever since 1934 – the year of publication of *Logische Syntax der Sprache* – Carnap himself sensed the impossibility of his 'antimetaphysical' programme: logical syntax does not fall under the proclaimed analyticity (§34d). Henceforth, as channelled by Quinean 'liberalism' (W.V.O.

priori), relentlessly insists on turning the concept into a 'pseudo-function' [*simili-fonction*] subject to the control of public criteria (the democratic test of clarity). The fact that the 'scientific' chapters of this thoroughly philosophical book take the form of a global debate with a certain 'Bergsonism' is not something we can afford to ignore. Despite the abundance of references to the theory of the two multiplicities, and despite the book's reprise of the distinction between real and actual, together with the omni-presence of the category of the virtual and of the theory of indi-viduation via a cascade of actualizations – so many themes endlessly reworked by Deleuze ever since his *Bergsonism* – the tone is set by the lapidary critique of Bergson's all too elemen-tary distribution between the 'ready made' or 'already done' [*tout fait*] and the 'in the making' or 'being done' [*se faisant*].[12] So much so that a painter's vision – Paul Klee's – 'was certainly more sound when he said that mathematics and physics, in addressing themselves to the functional, take not the completed form but formation itself as their object' (146/155). Truth be told, scientific multiplicities are less composed by 'sets' than they are dependent on functions, the function itself being thinkable only in terms of the *ordering of an 'in the making'* (variation, tem-poral modulation).[13] Therefore we should avoid limiting science

---

* (POST-)ANALYTICAL NOTE 2: (continued)
Quine, 'Two Dogmas of Empiricism', 1951: there is no principled distinction between analytical and synthetic propositions), 'the concept expressed by the expression "analytical philosophy" evades explicit definition' (P. Jacob). To put it otherwise: the logical universalism that underlies the values of 'clarity' and 'intersubjectivity' constitutive of the metaphilosophical practice of (post)ana-lytical philosophers will be nothing but a matter . . . of *style* (Récanati, Engel). Short of a return to the great tradition of American pragmatism (Peirce, James, Dewey), the reader will recognize in this whole story a considerable element of humour, which I would hesitate to call English.

[12] One of the earliest complete uses of the distinction occurs in Bergson's *Time and Free Will: An Essay on the Immediate Data of Consciousness*, trans. F.L. Pogson (Mineola, NY: Dover, 2001 [1913]), p. 119. – Make no mistake, none of the elements that make up this critique are really *new*. See in particular *Difference and Repetition*, p. 238. What preoccupies us here is determining the novel perception that now holds these elements together.

[13] See *The Fold: Leibniz and the Baroque*, p. 19, where Deleuze quotes the fol-lowing remark by Simondon: 'modulating is moulding in a continuous and per-petually variable fashion'.

to the *theorem*, which would entail claiming, a little hastily, the monopoly on problems for the field of philosophical creation. In science, *just as* in philosophy, the being of the problematic relates to that which 'gives' the progressive determination of the corresponding elements ('in the process of being determined' [127/133]). By the same token, we must avoid making *lived experience* [*vécu*] into the defining characteristic of the philosophical persona, as we do when we reduce the scientific observer to a mere *symbol* dependent on that persona: 'There is ideal perception and affection in both, but they are very different from each other' (126/132).[14]

The Bergsonian understanding of the distribution of the two sorts of 'multiplicity' – the scientific multiplicity of the determination of independent variables and the philosophical multiplicity of the expression of the inseparability of variations – is thereby put into question. Science, which relates to the chaotic virtual inasmuch as this virtual actualizes itself by slowing down, also follows lines of differentiation through the potential it appropriates, in the experience of a time not easily reducible to 'a fourth dimension of space'.[15] In truth, this time between two instants that Bergson sought to preserve does nothing but subjectively actualize a functional domain. By treating this time as 'a colourless shadow which pure duration projects into homogeneous space' and denouncing the 'contradictory idea of succession in simultaneity'[16] that science develops to the exclusive benefit of space, Bergson 'has still not left the domain of functions and introduces only a little of the lived into it' (149/157) – *or a little of history*, between two instants necessarily oriented

---

[14] [The preceding passage reads: 'It is not enough to assimilate the scientific observer [. . .] to a simple *symbol* that would mark states of variables, as Bergson does, while the philosophical persona would have the privilege of *the lived* (a being that endures) because he will undergo the variations themselves. The philosophical persona is no more lived experience than the scientific observer is symbolic' (125/132).]

[15] *Time and Free Will*, p. 109. On duration considered as 'the virtual insofar as it is actualized', see Deleuze's *Le bergsonisme* (Paris: PUF, 1966), especially p. 36; trans. Hugh Tomlinson and Barbara Habberjam as *Bergsonism* (New York: Zone Books, 1991), p. 42.

[16] *Time and Free Will*, pp. 231, 228.

according to a before and after, coming to occupy and intersect [*occuper et recouper*] a nature that finds its reference in the system of coordinates.

It is not the historical or historial passage of time that stands in opposition to the scientific order of time, as it descends by functions from the virtual to the states of affairs and bodies actualizing it; rather, it is the Event, 'or the part that eludes its own actualisation in everything that happens' (147/156). The event constitutes *another* virtual, which no longer distinguishes itself from the actual by its chaotic potentiality, but rather by its consistency and *incorporeal reality* 'on the plane of immanence which snatches it from chaos'. *And everything that follows*, from 'the event that is a meanwhile [*entre-temps*]' (149/158) where nothing happens but everything becomes, to its *counter-effectuation* 'whenever it is abstracted from states of affairs [in which it actualizes itself] so as to isolate its concept' (150–1/159), to the very position of philosophy vis-à-vis science ('climbing' and 'descending' along *two different lines*), derives from the reorientation of both thought and what thinking means which Deleuze discovered in the *Stoic irreduction* of incorporeal events – to the body on the one hand and *to universals on the other*. When it all rises back up to the surface to 'represent' any possible ideality (which is not without echoes of Spinozist immanence), and two readings of time, that of Chronos and that of Aion, confront one another.[17]

Aion is the truth of the event, 'pure empty form of time, which has freed itself of its present corporeal content', 'all the power of an "instant" which distinguishes its occurrence from any assignable present'.[18] As for Chronos: 1) We will be attentive first of all to the fact that it refers to the *process of incorporation*. Chronologically, to temporalize is to actualize: chronic time is inseparable from the movement of actualization. 2) In so doing,

---

[17] We know that *The Logic of Sense* proposes nothing less than an experimentation with these surface games which reflect the great Stoic duality. On the reference to the Stoics, see *What is Philosophy?*, p. 120/127. This rediscovery of the Stoics – beyond Bergson, via Spinoza (and Nietzsche) – is one of the book's deepest structuring principles. One could imagine no better illustration of the 'stratigraphic' time of superimposition that characterizes philosophy *in the making*.

[18] *The Logic of Sense*, 'Twenty-Third Series: Of the Aion', pp. 194,193/165.

its presentation is permanently threatened by a 'chaotic' becoming that complicates the composed unity of corporeal causes and tends to escape from the present measure of bodies ('the pure and measureless becoming of qualities threatens the order of qualified bodies from within').[19] 3) Whence *a revenge of the future and the past on the present, a revenge that Chronos must still express in terms of the present*, in terms that threaten its linear concatenation and imply the 'mixture'[20] of states of affairs and the communication of bodies.

We are not returning to these propositions in order to suggest a rapprochement – as anachronistic as it would be vain – tending towards the conclusion that Chronos would (already) express a time soon to be that of science. To recap, what is worth registering instead is the fact that the surpassing of Bergsonism *qua* tributary of a still hierarchical (and dialecticizable?) difference between science and philosophy is effectuated in a revaluation of the question of science *as inspired by Stoicism*.[21] Moreover, it is important to note that the Stoic inspiration behind *What is Philosophy?* reaches its strangest ontological resonance when the third ('chronic') moment is isolated. It is as if the serialization of time carried out by the scientific apparatus in the process of its paradigmatic self-comprehension – via a 'scientific progress' in which 'the before (the previous) always designates bifurcations and ruptures to come, and the after designates retroactive reconnections' (118/124) – necessarily had to exercise its capture *upon and on the basis of an unhinged present*, a present that has undergone the un-chained subversion of the future and the past and which in turn will give rise to new ruptures and bifurcations *before* they are projected into 'necessarily orientated systems of reference'. Orientation belongs to a re-composed present, standing as a judge over both past and

---

[19] *The Logic of Sense*, p. 192/164.

[20] Recall that in *What is Philosophy?* (144/152), the Stoic term 'mixture' [*mélange*] appears in order to qualify actualities constituted by states of affairs, as they exit from virtual chaos.

[21] Once again, it matters little whether it is possible to see the premises of this surpassing of Bergsonism 'ever since', say, *Difference and Repetition*. For my part, I am inclined to believe that Guattari's *schizoanalytic exercises* played a key role in the rediscovery of the 'scientific' potentialities of Stoicism.

future. Providing the key to history envisaged as a series or a re-
concatenation, the present also serves to seal the passionate
relationship of science with religion, 'as can be seen in all the
attempts at scientific uniformisation and universalisation in the
search for a single law, a single force, or a single interaction'
(118–9/125). This paradigmatic present, which submits the
appearance and production of the new to the rational economy
of a *global relation* between independent variables, is itself also
constituted 'by a spiritual tension rather than by a spatial intuition' (119/125).[22] *Qua* spiritual, this tension impresses into the
a priori form of time the standpoint of properly scientific
opinion (*Urdoxa*) on the internal chaosmos of science, from
which it retains only what it thinks it can *deduce* from 'initial
conditions'; *qua* material, this tension expresses the pressure
and resistance of becoming, its primacy over a state-form which
is 'indetermined', in fits and starts [*par à-coup*], by the variations of certain measured and corporeal presents that can no
longer be equated to one another within a global and homogenized present, but rather form so many partial presents relative
to the fluctuating singularities of the actualization of 'mix-
tures'.

　　Borne along by the need for a non-unitary genre of narration,
freed from the paradigmatic God of classical rationality, another
image of the history of the sciences emerges; an image criss-
crossed by forces that are the carriers of sense and of its transformation. What is the philosophy of the sciences? A logic of
forces affected by a heterologic of sense.

Is this to say that by systematically marking out this insight we
would be returning to the opposition between *two images of
science*, formalized by Deleuze and Guattari in *A Thousand
Plateaus*? That does not seem to be the case, because what
remains to be understood is, *quite the reverse*, why the reapprai-
sal of the relations between science and philosophy in these scientific chapters of *What is Philosophy?* does *not* allow for the
least reference to the two models and to the 'tension-limit

[22] How could Bergson be targeted at greater depth?

between the two kinds of science'[23]: *royal science* and *nomad science*, 'major science' and 'minor science' – a conception that opposes the legality of the state-form with a model of becoming and heterogeneity.

Rereading these pages of *What is Philosophy?*, the answer is all too clear. Relating the object of science back to its formation ('in the making') rather than to its finished form (the 'ready made') – with the two correlated notions of *potential* and *partial observer* – the extraction of the category of *function* obliges the authors to accentuate the interaction of these two figures of science to the detriment of their exteriority.[24] Without this interaction it is *practically* impossible to understand *the truly modern form of the autonomy of science*. This hypothesis is confirmed, not just once, but twice over. Recall that it is potential, as an *'absolutely indispensable correlate to the state of affairs'* (145/153, my emphasis), which takes charge of the 'accidents, adjunctions, ablations or even projections' that constitute so many 'problems' faced by the state of affairs – whilst it was these very affections that characterized, in *A Thousand Plateaus*, the problematic model of nomad science and its effects as a war machine (*'problemata* are the war machine itself'[25]) launched against the 'theorem-element' of State science. As for the partial observer, it takes upon itself that part of the sensible which was once the domain of the 'ambulant' sciences, whose movement was determined by

[23] Gilles Deleuze and Félix Guattari, *Mille Plateaux* (Paris: Les Éditions de Minuit, 1980), p. 450; *A Thousand Plateaus*, trans. Brian Massumi (Minneapolis: University of Minnesota Press, 1987), p. 365 (my emphasis).

[24] In *A Thousand Plateaus*, the account of the two genres of science was placed instead under the rubric of exteriority. Consider its Proposition III: 'The exteriority of the war machine is also attested to by epistemology, which intimates the existence and perpetuation of a "nomad" or "minor science"' (446/361). The heading would seem to foretell the trans-historical character of the reflections to come. But, as we shall see, the 'interactive' apprehension of these two *Idealtypen* is not foreign to the methods deployed in *A Thousand Plateaus*.

[25] *A Thousand Plateaus*, p. 448/362. Shortly before this remark Deleuze and Guattari write the following: 'the model [of nomad science] is problematic, rather than theorematic: figures are considered only from the viewpoint of the *affections* that befall them: sections, ablations, adjunctions, projections'. The same applies to the notions of 'singularities', 'proximity' and dimensions or 'supplementary events'.

their practice of *following* singularities, whilst the legal model limits itself to an 'ideal of reproduction' determined by 'the permanence of a fixed point of *view* that is external to what is reproduced'.[26]

But all this is turned upside down – already in *A Thousand Plateaus* itself, and despite the fact that the search for laws still 'savours of morality'[27] – thus showing how much more virtual or ideal than real is the opposition between the two kinds of science. On the very grounds of their submission to sensible and sensitive evaluations, nomad sciences refuse to lead science towards an autonomous power and development. Throwing up more problems than it can possibly resolve, this 'approximate knowledge' [*connaissance approchée*] is inevitably . . . problematic. As a result, it will be up to royal science to provide the scientific solution. Only royal science enjoys a metric power up to the task of constituting the 'autonomy of science [including the autonomy of experimental sciences]. That is why it is necessary to couple ambulant spaces with a space of homogeneity, without which the laws of physics would depend on particular points in space. But this is less a translation than a constitution: precisely that constitution the ambulant sciences did not undertake, and do not have the means to undertake'.[28] So it is that the discovery of continuous functions without derivatives can introduce a monstrous 'pathology' into mathematics, turning derivability into nothing more than a particular case. Nevertheless these remain functions, inasmuch as they break with the sensible conditions of the representation of natural intuition, relative both to space (a continuity in absolute fissure) and time (absolutely punctual, the present no longer has any meaning).[29] Briefly, without reterri-

[26] *A Thousand Plateaus*, p. 461/372.
[27] *A Thousand Plateaus*, p. 458/370. [Deleuze and Guattari are quoting Nietzsche here, 'I beware of speaking of chemical "laws": that savours of morality. It is rather a question of the absolute establishment of power relationships.' See *The Will to Power*, trans. Walter Kaufmann and R. J. Hollingdale (New York: Vintage Books, 1968), §630.]
[28] *A Thousand Plateaus*, p. 463/374. See also p. 607/486: 'Major science has a perpetual need for the inspiration of the minor; but the minor would be nothing if it did not confront and conform to the highest scientific requirements.'
[29] See Jean-Joseph Goux, 'Dérivable et indérivable', *Critique* (1970), reprinted in *Freud, Marx. Économie et symbolique* (Paris: Seuil, 1973), pp. 149–71; Gaston

torialization onto the categorematic apparatus of functions, 'differential operations would be compelled to follow the evolution of a phenomenon'.[30] As far as one can tell, this is not exactly the perspective towards which tends the theory of 'fractal objects', for instance. Though it opens the way 'to a *very general* mathematical theory of free spaces',[31] Benoit Mandelbrot's work does not lead one to *follow* the infinitely fissured aleatory flux of matter, but to *describe* its constitution by establishing the *measurable* character of the degree of irregularity and fragmentation of the figures under consideration.

From *A Thousand Plateaus* to *What is Philosophy?* there is not, contrary to what one might think, a 'regression' from a more polemical and less consensual reading of science. To the extent that the functional integration of the two poles, which characterizes the modern identity of science, allows us to grasp, at the level of the *reason of the sensible*, the back and forth movement of matter, 'sometimes [. . .] already enveloped in qualitative multiplicity, sometimes already developed in a metric "schema" that draws it outside of itself'[32] – the analysis 'progresses'. What is 'gained' is a *definition 'in tension' of the modern power of science, which sees integrated into its functional practice the force-field that constitutes it.* Thus, we don't think we're breaking any new ground by affirming that the logic of propositions, in its univocal determination of *already constituted* objects, to which it applies the empty reference of truth-value, has as its primary concern the need to neutralize the field of forces in the 'recognition of the true'. That is why logic is no less reductivist with regard to science (the 'logicization' of functives) than to philosophy (the 'propositionalization' of concepts).

Bachelard, *La Philosophie du non. Essai d'une philosophie du nouvel esprit scientifique* (Paris: PUF, 1940), ch. 6; finally, in order to complete our regressive list, let us mention Jean Perrin's remarkable preface to *Les Atomes* (Paris, 1913).

[30] *A Thousand Plateaus*, 463/374 [translation modified].

[31] *A Thousand Plateaus*, p. 607/486. I've added the italics to emphasize that it is precisely this *generality* which accounts for the scientific value (of the solution) to Mandelbrot's theory.

[32] *A Thousand Plateaus*, p. 604/484.

[33] *A Thousand Plateaus*, p. 463/374.

Allow me to venture a final comment, or perhaps better, a final question, before concluding this second phase of my commentary. Have we not *lost* something in this movement of functional sublation of the two genres of science, in particular on the side of the 'minor' invention of problems, whose solution referred back 'to a whole set of collective, non-scientific activities'?[33] Must a scientific solution – in order to be deemed 'major' and attain the incontestable maturity of autonomy – exclude *a priori* the pragmatic and 'political' dimension of its assemblages of enunciation and experimentation? 'Certainly', one will reply, since this is precisely the image of science that science itself wishes to communicate. But in this way, the risk increases of having exchanged the speculative arrogance of philosophy (judging science) for the ideographic recognition of a science that judges its own procedures in the name of a bond between rationality and the power of the function, a bond so exclusive that by virtue of the distinction between science and non-science it ends up impeding any interrogation of the material and institutional arrangements [*dispositifs*] that condition the production of scientific statements. If it is true that these descriptions only count provided they do not claim to account for the conditions of existence of a science (*the doxological illusion*), they nevertheless have the merit of combating the inverse illusion, which consists in imagining that, at a certain degree of formalization, the laws of construction of a given science 'are at the same time and with full title conditions of existence' (*the formalist illusion*). One step further and we would have to admit that in order to think science, it is *necessary*:

> Above all, [. . .] to give free rein to two forms of extrapolation which have symmetrical and inverse reductive role. *Epistemological* extrapolation [and] *genetic* extrapolation. . . . In one case, the science is given the responsibility of explaining its own historicity; in the other, various historical determinations are required to explain a scientificity. But this is to ignore the fact that the place in which a science appears and unfolds is neither this science itself distributed according to a teleological sequence, nor a set of mute practices or extrin-

---

[34] Michel Foucault, 'Sur l'archéologie des sciences. Réponse au Cercle

sic determinations, but the field of knowledge with the set of relations which traverse it.[34]

In *What is Philosophy?* – and this is without doubt where the book's speculative daring is at its highest, where we encounter its *omphalos* or *complicatio* – this movement of re-cognizing the constituent and transformative dimensions of knowledge undergoes a process of involution, turning into the metaphysical discovery of an 'non-objectifiable' brain that can no longer be treated as a 'constituted object of science' (a determinate function), a brain that becomes 'subject' within an infinite field of forces in which *all the problems of interference between planes* must be taken up again *from another point of view*: from the brain as heterogenesis of thought to 'thought as heterogenesis' (188/199).

d'épistémologie', *Cahiers pour l'analyse* 9 (1968), especially pp. 35–8. Reprinted in *Dits et Écrits* (Paris: Gallimard, 2001), pp. 724–59. Translated into English by Robert Hurley as 'On the Archaeology of the Sciences: Response to the Epistemology Circle', in *Essential Works of Michel Foucault*, vol. 2, ed. James D. Faubion (London: Allen Lane/Penguin, 1998), pp. 330, 327.

III   Onto-Ethologics

The patch tends to bring hermeneutics to a halt because it offers nothing but quasi, *that is displacements, metonyms, metamorphoses [. . .]. In this regard, the patch presents a risk for thought, but this is the very risk of painting, as it comes forward, as it takes a stand: because when the matter of representation comes forward, the entire realm of the represented risks collapsing. However, interpretation has no choice but to acknowledge this risk, in order to take stock of it, to measure up to it, to point to – if only to point to – the 'intractable' that its object constitutes.*

Georges Didi-Huberman

All of a sudden, there opens up another point of view – that of an ontogenesis whose conditions of exercise require undoing the dependence of the point of view on a preformed subject, whether as *terminus a quo* or *sub-ject*. As Deleuze puts it in *The Fold*: 'on the contrary, a subject will be what comes to the point of view, or rather what inhabits the point of view'[1] – and in this habitation the subject becomes; it is projected between the physical depths and the metaphysical surface where all events are inscribed. *The Thought-Brain is the milieu of this becoming that the subject produces when the brain becomes subject*, or intellect

---

[1] *The Fold*, p. 27/19 [translation modified]. ['Inhabits' here translates *demeure*, which could also be rendered as 'remains' or even 'is', and, in noun form (*la demeure*), could give 'dwelling-place', or 'residence'.]

– an agent intellect in a state of 'acquisition' by the material intellect[2] under the three aspects of philosophy, science and art. The
mental objects of these three aspects will be localized 'in the
deepest of the synaptic fissures, in the hiatuses, intervals and
meantimes of an nonobjectifiable brain, in a place where to go in
search of them will be to create. [. . .] It is the brain that thinks
and not man – the latter being only a cerebral crystallisation'
(197–8/209–10). *Homo non intelligit . . .*[3]

Or, to paraphrase Whitehead – whose philosophy of the organism 'surveys', as we shall see, the concluding pages of *What is
Philosophy?* – we could say that man is a cerebral *prehension*,
actualizing the prehending subject which is the *superject* of its
experiences of thought. It is thus that, taken at the simplest level,
his 'philosophy of experience' reverses the customary order and
conceives of thought as the operation that constitutes the
thinker, who is constituted in this 'occasion' (what Whitehead
calls *the occasional thinker*): 'The thinker is the final end whereby
there is the thought. In this inversion we have the final contrast
between a philosophy of substance and a philosophy of the
organism. The operations of an organism are directed towards
the organism as a "superject" and are not directed from the
organism as a 'subject' [. . .]. They are "vectors".'[4]

---

[2] This is an approximate translation of the *intellectus adeptus agens*, such as
it appeared to Albertus Magnus, that great reader of Averroès: as the Latin
version of Alexander of Aphrodisias' 'materialised monopyschism,' which 'presents a purely naturalised version of immanence'. See Alain de Libera, *Albert le
Grand et la philosophie* (Paris: Vrin, 1990), pp. 222–32 and pp. 253–62 for the
philological explanation of 'Alexander's' formula.

[3] According to the generic formula of Medieval monopsychism, which we
would like to link here to the affirmation of a speculative naturalism, even
though 'we no longer believe in a whole as interiority of thought – even an open
one; we believe in a force from the outside which hollows itself out, grabs us and
attracts the inside', Deleuze, *Cinéma 2. L'Image-temps* (Paris, Minuit, 1985), p.
276; *Cinema 2: The Time-Image*, trans. Hugh Tomlinson and Robert Galeta
(London: Athlone, 1989), p. 212.

[4] Alfred North Whitehead, *Process and Reality. An Essay in Cosmology* (New
York: The Free Press, 1978), p. 151; in the same way, the sentient being is a unity
emergent from its own sensations. On the 'accidental' character of clear and distinct thought with regard to 'human experience', see *Modes of Thought* (Free
Press, 1968), pp. 156–8. The fundamental point remains the negation of all

If we take that into consideration, Whitehead's critique of the philosophical tradition is among the most easily understood. As he explains, in its 'substantialist' tendencies the tradition has done nothing but deduce the conditions of existence of substance from 'the macroscopic objects of experience'.[5] Against this metaphysics of substance, which excludes the becoming of the nature of things in favour of the sole *transition* from whence originates the power of the past as sufficient reason of the present, Whitehead proposes a 'metaphysics of flux', of a flux inherent to the 'microscopic' (or molecular . . .) constitution of the world and of the particular existent, which he calls 'concrescence'. Concrescence qualifies the process of 'grasping'[6] by which the multiple synthesizes itself into an original unity; it makes every 'actual entity' into the act of a becoming. This becoming in turn refers back to a point of view as the condition under which a 'subject' prehends a variation which expresses the entire world from a single perspective. That is because the prehended is itself an antecedent or concomitant prehension, so that every prehension is a prehension of a prehension and every actual entity is an acting entity. Furthermore, every act becomes, insofar as it is a concrescence of prehensions, an actual individual entity vibrating in unison with the cosmos . . . The term 'sensation' (or 'feeling') will serve as a generic description of those operations whereby a unity of experiences (an 'actual occasion')

metaphysical dualism, which is deemed responsible for blinding both science *and* modern philosophy (Descartes); it is this critique which gives rise to the philosophy of the organism. Remember the definitive formulation in *Adventures in Ideas* (Free Press, 1967), p. 253: 'Consciousness is a variable element which flickers uncertainly on the surface of experience.'

[5] See *Process and Reality*, pp. 157–8: 'the subjectivist principle follows from three premises: i) the acceptance of the "substance-quality" concept as expressing the ultimate ontological principle; ii) the acceptance of Aristotle's definition of a primary substance, as always a subject and never a predicate; iii) the assumption that the experient subject is a primary substance'. It is with Descartes that the metaphysics of 'substance-quality' affirms itself in an exclusive and absolute fashion (p. 137).

[6] Recall that Guattari's concept of the 'grasping existential' is elaborated in direct and constant reference to the work of Whitehead – see *Cartographies schizo-analytiques* (Paris: Galilée, 1989), p. 82; and of course, *Chaosmose*, pp. 155–60. (Incidentally, this term 'grasp' doesn't appear in any of the indexes of Whiteheadian concepts that I've had the opportunity to consult).

grasps the entire universe under a unity of apperception – *which one could just as well call a micro-brain. This comes down to putting sensation into the world, and the world within the subject emerging from it ('a 'superject' rather than a 'subject')*[7] – recognizing in the prehended *datum* the existence of sensation as a *vector* of physical quantities, *prior to their classical (scalar) scientific coordination*[8]: 'The key notion from which such construction should start is that the energetic activity considered in physics is the emotional activity entertained in life.'[9]

In brief, what Deleuze and Guattari 'find' in Whitehead, viewed as the speculative heir to the empiricist tradition, is a superior sensualism founded on an experimental ontological principle that – between science and philosophy – countereffectuates the Copernican revolution by undermining its epistemological base. The question is no longer that of the *methodological* dependence of the object in relation to the subject, but of the *ontological* auto-constitution of a new subject on the basis of its objects. 'In Whitehead, the standard transcendental subject is a physical entity, just like its objects.' For Jean-Claude Dumoncel, this means that 'Whitehead thereby opens up a promised land for the philosopher that he had no longer dared hope for: the prospect of a *transcendental philosophy without idealism!*'[10] The *reformed subjectivist principle* states that if the

---

[7] *Process and Reality*, p. 88.

[8] *Process and Reality*, p. 177, '*The philosophy of organism attributes "feeling" throughout the actual world [. . .]. The dominance of the scalar physical quantity, inertia, in the Newtonian physics obscured the recognition of the truth that all fundamental physical quantities are vector and not scalar*.' This 'truth' is that of the theory of quanta which endows 'nature' with an exclusively vectorial structure (see the question of the vibratory production of energy as envisaged in *Science and the Modern World* [London: Macmillan, 1925], chapter 8). Remember too that Samuel Butler's great book on Transformationism, *Life and Habit*, from 1878, is prefaced with a free translation of the following lines from Lucian's *Icaromenippus*, sections 21–22: 'Will you remember to tell Zeus all this? And you may add that I cannot remain at my post unless he will pulverize the physicists, muzzle the logicians, raze the Porch, burn the Academy and put an end to the strolling in the Lyceum. That might secure me a little peace from these daily mensurations. – I will remember, said I', *The Works of Lucian of Samosata*, 4 vols., trans. H.W. Fowler and F.G. Fowler (Oxford: Clarendon Press, 1905).

[9] Whitehead, *Modes of Thought*, p. 168.

[10] Jean-Claude Dumoncel, 'Whitehead ou le cosmos torrentiel. Introduction

object is the correlate of the experiencing or prehending subject
('*the primary* datum *is "the subject experiencing its objects as"*
. . .'), there is no reason to abstractly isolate impressions *qua*
data.[11]

The secret of Whitehead's 'panpsychism' is that in it transcendental philosophy becomes a *micro-metaphysics* of real experience. The manner in which this panpsychism leads to a *material meta-aesthetic*[12] is explored by Deleuze and Guattari in *What is Philosophy?*

critique à une lecture de *Process and Reality*', *Archives de philosophie* 47 (1984), p. 584. It is therefore impossible to imagine a more 'inoperative' critique than the one proposed by Tom Rockmore, who bemoans the absence of a 'moment of self-consciousnes [. . .] or introspection [. . .] so dominant in German Idealism' (in 'Whitehead et Hegel. Réalisme, idéalisme et philosophie spéculative', *Archives de philosophie* (April–June 1990), p. 269; published in English as 'Realism, Idealism, and Speculative Philosophy', in *Hegel and Whitehead: Contemporary Perspectives on Systematic Philosophy*, ed. G.R. Lucas [Albany: SUNY Press, 1986]).

[11] See *Process and Reality*: 'Kant, following Hume, assumes the radical disconnection of impressions *qua data*; and therefore conceives his transcendental aesthetic to be mere description of a subjective process appropriating the data by orderliness of feeling. The philosophy of organism aspires to construct a critique of pure feeling [. . .]' (p. 113). And further: 'The difficulties of all schools of modern philosophy lie in the fact that, having accepted the subjectivist principle, they continue to use philosophical categories derived from another point of view' (pp. 166–7). The general formula for the *reformed subjectivist principle* is 'Process is the becoming of experience.' See also *Adventures of Ideas*: 'An occasion of experience which includes a human mentality is an extreme instance, at one end of the scale, of those happenings which constitute nature [. . .] The notion of physical energy, which is at the base of physics, must then be conceived as an abstraction from the complex energy, emotional and purposeful, inherent in the subjective form of the final synthesis in which each occasion completes itself' (pp. 184, 186).

[12] It is not an indifferent matter that this expression emerges in Deleuze in the context of a commentary on the *Critique of Judgment*, see *La Philosophie critique de Kant* (Paris: PUF, 1963), p. 83; *Kant's Critical Philosophy: The Doctrine of the Faculties*, trans. Hugh Tomlinson and Barbara Habberjam (Minneapolis: Minnesota University Press, 1985), p. 57. One should also note that the reference to *Process and Reality* – considered as one of the 'greatest books of modern philosophy' – appears in *Difference and Repetition* (pp. 364–5/284–5) in the midst of a 'post-Kantian' discussion of the question of the reunion (one does not dare to say 'reunification') of the two 'parts of the Aesthetic which have been so unfortunately separated, the theory of the forms of experience and that of the work of art as experimentation'. – For Whitehead's 'aesthetics', the reader should refer above all to *Science and the Modern World* (New York: The Free Press, 1967 [1925]), ch. 5, where the author provides a very close analysis of the

Whitehead, or the vitalist celebration of a 'pure internal Awareness' [*pur sentir interne*] constituting 'a single plane of composition bearing all the varieties of the universe' (201/213), 'where sensation is formed by contracting that which composes it and by composing itself with other sensations that contract it in turn. [. . .] Sensation fills out the plane of composition and is filled with itself by filling itself with what it contemplates: it is "enjoyment" and "self-enjoyment".[13] It is a subject, or rather an *inject* [. . .] no causality is intelligible without this subjective instance. [. . .] Everywhere there are forces that constitute micro-brains, or an inorganic life of things' (199–200/212–3).

Contrariwise, and proceeding from the *collective brain* – itself constituted by the prehensive unification which is the very ground of nature – in order to attain the material brain, we must concur with Whitehead that the cerebral surface 'is continuous with the body and the body is continuous with the rest of the world. Human experience is an act of self-origination including the whole of nature, limited to the perspective of a focal region located within the body, *but not necessarily persisting in any fixed coordination with a definite part of the brain*'.[14]

If we follow this shift, the cognitivist hypothesis that consists in putting a given cognitive function in relation to its neural organization and its corresponding state of activity – thus turning the brain into a *logical object* – falls under what Whitehead calls the *fallacy of misplaced concreteness and simple location*, the very basis of the Galilean system of nature. In cognitivism, everything happens *as if* it sufficed to speak of cerebral *states* for the functioning of the brain to allow itself to be defined – *at one and the same time* – in terms of the paradigm of deduc-

Footnote 12 (*continued*)
reaction of English romanticism (Wordsworth, Shelley . . .) against the abstract materialism of Galilean science. The conclusion is the following: in fact, and in accordance with our perceptual experience, 'nature cannot be divorced from its aesthetic values; and [. . .] these values arise from the cumulation, in some sense, of the brooding presence of the whole on to in its various parts' (pp. 87–8). See also *Adventure of Ideas*, ch. 18.

[13] Whitehead speaks of *satisfaction*, specifying it pertains to the ultimate character of the unity of sensation of an actual entity, see *Adventures of Ideas*, p. 166.

[14] *Adventures of Ideas*, p. 255 (my emphasis).

tive logic *and* as a dynamic object (symbols being both signifying and material).[15]

But has it been sufficiently remarked upon that philosophers are no longer alone in claiming that the brain, 'treated as a constituted object of science, can be an organ only of the formation and communication of opinion' (197/209) – 'a system of abstractions, admirably expressing the interests of the time', according to Whitehead's words, which find here a hitherto unexpected domain of application?

Often cited by Guattari, Francisco J. Varela, for instance, is preoccupied with demarcating himself from the cognitivist axiom by studying the aptitude to self-organization evinced by the rhizomatic arrangements of neural networks.[16] Varela remarks that the 'emergent properties' based on the dense network of interconnections that constitutes the brain can make all its components resonate without requiring any central processing unit to control the brain's functioning (or, of the brain as multiplicity: 'a noisy cocktail party conversation rather than [. . .] a chain of command'). Besides, the introduction of the notion of 'attractor' testifies to the bridges that are beginning to emerge between the different levels of description of natural, artificial and cognitive phenomena. Generally speaking, 'arborised paradigms give way to rhizomatic figures, acentred systems, networks

[15] Here it is worth picking up again Whitehead's *Science and the Modern World*, ch. 4. In two divergent ways, this point of view has been developed recently by Jean-Claude Milner in the *Annuaire philosophique*, 1988–1989 (Paris: Seuil, 1989), pp. 199–219 (a review of Francisco Varela's *Connaître. Les sciences cognitives, tendances et perspectives*); and by Isabelle Stengers, in 'Et si demain le cerveau . . .', *Annales de l'Institut de philosophie de l'université de Bruxelles* (1991), pp. 147–61. On the 'secret pact' between the cognitivist and connectionist paradigms – 'with this difference that cognitivism wishes to think the brain in the image of the computer and connectionism the computer in the image of the brain' – a digital brain supposed to provide the foundations of their shared functionalism – see François Rastier, *Sémantique et recherches cognitives* (Paris: PUF, 1991), ch. 1. For a more balanced approach to connectionism, see Varela's works cited below.

[16] On the brain as rhizomatic, acentred system see Deleuze and Guattari, *A Thousand Plateaus*, pp. 24–6/15–6; Deleuze, *The Time-Image*, p. 274/278; *Pourparlers*, (Paris: Minuit, 1990), p. 204; *Negotiations*, trans. Martin Joughin (New York: Columbia University Press, 1994), p. 149. The key reference here is Steven Rose, *The Conscious Brain* (New York: Knopf, 1975).

of finite automatons, chaoid states' (204/216). In Varela, the notion of representation will be severely undermined ('since only a predetermined world can be represented') in the name of the concept of *enaction* – a concept we shall risk inscribing into the Whiteheadian current of thought, in spite of the hermeneutico-phenomenological origin proclaimed by its advocate.[17] This is because, from the perspective of autonomy and autopoiesis, system and world emerge at the same time: 'the subject and object are each other's reciprocal and simultaneous prerequisite and precondition. In philosophical terms, knowing is ontological'.[18]

On the basis of this hypothesis, we can no longer limit ourselves to the affirmation that *there exist* (as a logical form) in the subject *a priori* forms whose coherence with the brute data of the world is adequately verified by experience. What now needs to be grasped is precisely the first figure of this experience, on the basis of which being as subject and being as object constitute themselves in the reciprocity of knowledge and action ('embodiment'). This emergence of mind appears as the relation – qualified by Simondon as *transductive* – between world and self [*moi*]. We can still ask ourselves whether the phenomenological interpretation of the 'making emerge' (*hervorbringen*) – which is not always convincing within the scientific domain in which Varela's theory wishes to play a functional role (see the thesis of 'operational closure'[19]) – is capable of retracing the *ontogenesis*

[17] Varela quotes Heidegger, Gadamer and especially the first Merleau-Ponty, the author of *The Structure of Behaviour*, in his book (co-authored with Evan Thompson and Elisabeth Rosch) *The Embodied Mind: Cognitive Science and Human Experience* (Cambridge, MA: The MIT Press, 1991), Intro and ch. 8.

[18] Francisco J. Varela, *Connaître. Les sciences cognitives, tendances et perspectives* (Paris: Seuil, 1989), pp. 75, 92, 99. [This book is a translation of Varela's *Cognitive Science: A Cartography of Current Ideas* (New York/Leuven: Pergamon Press/Leuven University Press, 1988).] – Guattari's ontological pragmatics will make frequent use of this basic idea: 'that before every categorisation of representation in terms of objectivity and subjectivity, a point of view is an act and, at the very least, the prefiguring of an energised interaction', see *Cartographies schizoanalytiques*, pp. 209–10.

[19] Francisco J. Varela, *Autonomie et connaissance. Essai sur le vivant* (Paris: Seuil, 1989). The essentials of this thesis had been presented in *Principles of Biological Autonomy* (New York: Elsevier, 1979).

of the ontological nature of knowledge and of its organ 'which constructs worlds rather than reflecting them'. The problem is thus no longer that of analysing how the 'organ of form' evolves as a function of the establishment of cognitive interactions with the co-implicated environment, but rather of marking what its being-in-the-world, such as it actualizes itself in the approach of the discovering mind, necessarily presupposes.

All that's left is to repeat here Gilbert Simondon's demonstration, mindful of the attention that Deleuze never ceased to grant this body of work ever since *Difference and Repetition*. Following Simondon, we can say of the movement of *this* approach, of the movement of discovery, that it:

> consists in *following being in its genesis*, in accomplishing the genesis of thought in parallel with that of the object, [since] each thought, each conceptual discovery [. . .] is a reprise of the first individuation [. . .], of which it provides a distant resonance, partial but faithful. [Conclusion:] According to this perspective, ontogenesis would become the starting point for philosophical thought, it would really constitute first philosophy [. . .], prior to objective knowledge, which is a relation of the individual being to its milieu after individuation. Prior to any critique of knowledge [*connaissance*] comes the knowledge [*savoir*] of ontogenesis. Ontogenesis precedes critique and ontology.[20]

Or, to put it another way: the fact that ontology only precedes the critique of knowledge by being conditioned in turn by this

---

[20] Gilbert Simondon, *L'individuation psychique et collective* (Paris: Aubier, 1989), pp. 26, 127, 163. This means that the ontological difference as conceived by Heidegger, since it is still 'ensnared in secular dualisms', could never be primary . . . In this respect, see J. Garelli's elegant analysis in *Rhythmes et mondes. Au revers de l'identité et de l'altérité* (Grenoble: Jérome Millon, 1991), pp. 138–208, 216–22, 267–329. Having noted that Simondon's work is dedicated to Merleau-Ponty, Garelli quotes this note from June 1960: 'Show that philosophy as interrogation [. . .] can consist only in showing how the world is articulated starting from a zero of being which is not nothingness', *The Visible and the Invisible*, ed. Claude Lefort, trans. Alphonso Lingis (Evanston, IL: Northwestern University Press, 1990), p. 260. This will lead Merleau-Ponty in his last texts to conceive of ontology as 'intra-ontology' and to understand intentionality as being. This is nothing other than the point of departure for Simondon's reflection.

critique (this is as manifest in Duns Scotus as it is in Spinoza, *univocité oblige*, albeit according to perfectly dissymmetrical perspectives) *exposes* it to an ontogenesis that irrevocably conditions the question of being. From top to bottom, it will no longer be possible to pose the question in terms of the being [*être*] of the individuated being [*étant*]; the question will have to transfer its focus to a being in a phase of individuation, according to the perspective of a proto-ontic flux on whose basis alone can individuated ontic permanence (ek-sistants and beings) momentarily be gained. Correlatively, since being-in-the-world will only be attained *within* the individuation without a principle of the *being-of-the-world*, the process of individuation will no longer let itself be grasped in terms of the structure of ipseity of a falsely originary *Dasein* enveloping the world in its embrace. In my view, Deleuze and Guattari propose to call *brain* that *operation of being* that composes the meta-stable system of phases belonging to a pre-individual world in formation – in the midst of individuation – *qua ontogenesis of itself*. Following the principle of a conversion of the cerebral surface into a metaphysical surface,[21] we could almost say that the brain is ontology delivered over to the pragmatics *of* being.

To the degree that knowledge of this ontogenesis takes as its object an understanding of the ontological character of knowledge itself, it will be up to a 'first philosophy' to express the dimensionality of being as it individuates itself *qua* brain, by installing itself neither in the for-itself nor in the in-itself, but rather in the joint of being, in the pure form of the determinable . . . The brain, or that whereby a certain mode of self-affection and self-conditioning of being exists: autopoietic nucleus or fold, absolute surface possessing itself, auto-constitution of a form field, entailing the institution of a relation of reciprocity between the domain of the simultaneous and that of the successive, a relation that could be termed reflection[22] and which proceeds by

---

[21] Catalysed by the reading of Simondon and Ruyer, this path had been sketched out in *The Logic of Sense*, p. 259, footnote 3/355–6, footnote 3.

[22] Simondon, p. 149: 'Suppose that pure biological reality were to be constituted by the non-reciprocity of the relationship between the domain of simultaneity and that of the successive, whilst psychological reality is precisely the

survey of the entire field. Here one can glimpse the becoming-subject of a form-taking that 'potentializes', like an infinite speed (simultaneous succession), the internal resonance of being in relation to itself (what Ruyer calls *action according to an absolute surface*; but every form as such is the bearer of an energetic potential, as Guattari reminds us[23]). In short, in the form of being as relation, whilst transformation precedes information, the brain is the mind itself. Ontogenesis of the whole subject in the brain, a field of consciousness; and consciousness is *nothing other than form or, rather, active formation in its absolute existence*: consciousness and morphogenesis are one and the same thing.[24]

Let us now examine, dispensing with any further commentary, 'what are the characteristics of this brain, which is no longer defined by connections and secondary integrations? It is not a brain behind the brain but, first of all, a state of survey without distance, at ground level, a self-survey [. . .]. It is a primary, "true form" as Ruyer defined it: neither a Gestalt nor a perceived form but a *form in itself* that does not refer to any external point of

introduction of the reciprocity that we call "reflection".' The finest formula in this regard belongs to Merleau-Ponty, who invoked a *relief of the simultaneous and of the successive* in *The Visible and the Invisible*, p. 114.

[23] Related back to Hjelmslev, who stipulated the reversibility of forms of expression and of content, the 'formalist' claim is omnipresent in Guattari's work; see in particular *Cartographies schizo-analytiques*, pp. 116–7 and 234. The Hjelmslevian *identity* of forms of expression and content allows Guattari clearly to show that the question of the production of subjectivity is a function of the primacy of what he called 'the path of self-reference'; it is related to a processual subjectivity which installs itself transversally to the stratifications of power and knowledge (see the section entitled 'Liminaire' in *Cartographies schizo-analytiques*). Foucault addresses the problem entirely otherwise: starting out from the *relations of forces* between form of expression and form of content, he concludes by breaking through the Power-Knowledge axis by discovering the new dimension of *relation to self* [*rapport à soi*] (subjectivation).

[24] See Raymond Ruyer, *La genèse des formes vivantes*, (Paris: Flammarion, 1958), pp. 237–40: 'But, naturally, this consciousness, or this cerebral morphogenesis, is only a particular, derived case of organic consciousness and morphogenesis' (so much so that 'what appears to the physicist as a link made through an exchange of energy is nothing but an elementary field of consciousness'). Moreover, 'man is conscious, intelligent and inventive only because every living individuality is conscious, intelligent and inventive'; see respectively pp. 238–9, 243 and 255. Do we need to insist on the importance of the reference to Whitehead in all of Ruyer's work?

view [. . .] it is an absolute consistent form that surveys *itself* independently of any supplementary dimension [. . .] which remains
copresent to all its determinations without proximity or distance,
traverses them at infinite speed, without limit-speed, and which
makes of them so many *inseparable variations* on which it confers
an equipotentiality without confusion. We have seen that this
was the status of the concept . . .' (198/210) – from the point of
view, therefore, of a first philosophy *expressing* the primacy of
the brain in its pragmatic ontological dimension through the
creation of *self-determining* concepts.

(In this regard, Deleuze and Guattari's philosophy is perhaps
close to the new 'thinking' conceptuality required in Kant by the
productive function of reflective judgements in their relation to
the ontological dimension of 'aesthetic ideas': this conceptuality
should be grasped in the manner of a *'pure form'* entertaining a
privileged relationship with the infinite. Though it is hardly necessary to recall Deleuze's insistence regarding the originary and
founding character of aesthetic common sense – which enables
the free play of the imagination and understanding: 'A faculty
would never take on a legislative and determining role were not
all the faculties together in the first place capable of this free subjective harmony'[25] – it is worth recalling that reflective aesthetic
judgement belongs to the faculty of cognition [*connaître*] *which
it makes possible* by operating, according to its creative dimension, without a concept *given in advance*.)

At this level, still too abstract and yet so concrete (towards a
philosophy of the concrete . . .[26]), we can anticipate how the
primary consciousness on the basis of which this first philosophy
deploys itself is going to rub against the grain of *the* 'consciousness *of* . . .' so beloved of the phenomenology that is mobilized
around the problematic of *In-der-Welt-Sein* . . . Did that phenomenology not in fact intend to found its juridical priority over the
entirety of modern philosophy by arguing that the latter was only
a theory of knowledge, of the knowing subject in its relation to

[25] Gilles Deleuze, *Kant's Critical Philosophy*, p. 72/50.
[26] [*Vers le concret* (Towards the concrete), was the title of a book by Jean Wahl,
one of the first treatments in France of the philosophy of Whitehead, as well as
of American pragmatism.]

the known object, which neglected the making-appear of the appearance of the world 'itself': the invisible *of* this world? It matters little here that the phenomenological reduction remained ensnared in a transcendental consciousness by retrieving the problem of foundation according to an eminently Platonic scansion . . . Or that phenomenology 'radically established and methodically conducted', cannot but be metaphysical[27]; or is even, in Lévinas's words, a simple 'play of light'. The important thing is to be able to situate oneself with regard to phenomenology, which claims to grasp perception as the originary mode of the givenness [*donation*] of things themselves (the *flesh of* perception), in the same way that phenomenology situated itself with respect to Cartesianism – as a derived or 'degenerate' enterprise, usurping the radical character of its 'originariness', because it was not able to renounce the symbolic primacy of the individuality thematized

[27] Dominique Janicaud et al., *Phenomenology and the Theological Turn: The French Debate* (New York: Fordham University Press, 2001). – For a more detailed analysis of the slide from the methodological to the metaphysical concept of *Konstitution* in Husserl, see the writings of Ludwig Landgrebe. In the wake of the Dreyfus-McIntyre exchange on Husserl (see Hubert L. Dreyfus, 'Introduction' in *Husserl, Intentionality, and Cognitive Science* [Cambridge, MA: The MIT Press/Bradford Books, 1982] and Ronald McIntyre, 'Husserl and the Representational Theory of Mind', *Topoi* 5 [1986], pp. 101–13, reprinted in *Historical Foundations of Cognitive Science*, ed. J.-C. Smith [Boston: Kluwer, 1990]; the debate was translated and restaged in French in the journal *Études philosophiques* under the heading 'Phénoménologie et psychologie cognitive', January–March 1991), Elisabeth Rigal has opened up a particularly interesting area of research by relating (1) the metaphysical nature of the overcoming of consciousness defined as the consciousness-of-something in the absoluteness of the living present to (2) the analytical groundwork of the *Logical Investigations*, regarding which Husserl would have tried to *erase its traces rather than confront them*. This makes one think (3) that Husserlian metaphysics partially constituted itself in the attempt 'to appropriate the legacy it inherited from logical objectivism whilst annulling the internal tensions' derived from it. See Elisabeth Rigal 'Quelques remarques sur la lecture cognitiviste de Husserl', *Les Études philosophiques*, January–March 1991, p. 114. In this article one will re-encounter a displaced version of Foucault's intuition at the end of *The Birth of the Clinic: An Archaeology of Medical Perception*, trans. A.M. Sheridan Smith (London: Tavistock, 1973): 'that with which phenomenology was to oppose [positivism] so tenaciously was already present in its underlying structures [*le système de ses conditions*] [. . .]. So much so that contemporary thought, believing that it has escaped it since the end of the nineteenth century, has merely rediscovered, little by little, that which made it possible' (p. 199).

as *Dasein* and *Selbstheit* in the constitution of the world.
(Heidegger himself admitted he had failed to master the problem
of the coming-into-the-world of . . . *Dasein*.) How could this be
otherwise, if the primary form of consciousness, before *becoming*
consciousness-of, *is* form – that is *every* active formation in its
absolute existence and activity as form's self-possession – and if
every formation *is* consciousness immanent to the proto-ontic
field and, by this reason alone, irreducible to the 'ideal essences' of
a Husserlian *phänomenologische Psychologie*? That is why, if every
being and every form is its own subject (auto-subjectivity), 'consciousness and life are one and the same', 'the difference between
morphogenesis and noogenesis [is] ultimately superficial'.[28] This
is what we have collected here under the heading of *ontogenesis*,
suggesting, at the antipodes of a phenomenology more essential-
ist than material,[29] the rigorous programme of a *metaphysical
materialism* – provided that 'metaphysical' is accorded the precise
sense of a 'non-geometric dimension', of a 'non-spatial region' or
of a 'trans-spatial ideal', 'because the visible brain in space is only
the site of application of non-mechanical *feedbacks* to non-spatial
themes and ideals'.[30]

So we will not reply (any more?) to the question 'what is philosophy?', without retracing this movement, which is that of the
*ontogenesis of thought qua individuating becoming of being
[devenir d'individuation de l'être]*; without investing this form

---

[28] Ruyer, pp. 260, 262. That is why 'the consciousness that inheres in formation is not the consciousness *of* formation, whether as *lumen naturale* or as
intention directed at this formation. Primary consciousness is not consciousness
of . . .' (p. 240). No more so than 'self-survey' [*auto-survol*] is self-perception; see
Ruyer's *Néo-finalisme* (Paris: PUF, 1952), pp. 214–6, for the critique of the
Merleau-Ponty of *The Structure of Behaviour*. I have taken up all of these question again in *De l'impossibilité de la phénoménologie*, in accordance with the
principle of an axiom of complementarity between the 'phenomenology' of the
failure of logical formalism and the 'analysis' of the rupture of intentionality of
phenomenology.

[29] [The allusion here is to Michel Henry, *Phénoménologie matérielle* (Paris:
PUF, 1990).]

[30] Ruyer, p. 242. The best introduction to the 'non-spatial' is found in Ruyer's
La Cybernétique et l'origine de l'information (Paris: Flammarion, 1954), ch. 3.
The essential idea of this work is that the trans-spatio-temporal defines a poten-
tial with great precision. See also Ruyer's *Éléments de psycho-biologie* (Paris:
PUF, 1946), Introduction.

which is that of the brain becoming subject at the moment when it poses the concept as its first object. And it is up to philosophy to affirm itself as *this* infinite movement of coming and going, of eternal return, which does not project itself into the image of thought without returning as the matter of being: Thought and Nature, *Physis* and *Noûs*, the two faces of the plane of immanence traced by the brain as it maintains itself in the being it becomes (*superject*). Likewise, the morphogenesis of form in itself will also be accompanied by an energetics of force for itself. This force does not act, but holds itself in a kind of retreat; it creates the retreat implied by the survey, contracting 'the vibrations of the stimulant on a nervous surface or in a cerebral volume', a *sensation in itself* which is the index of becoming. Situated on a plane more fundamental than that of the mechanisms, dynamisms and finalities at work in the register of a localized causality, sensation is the correlate of the concept; 'it is no less brain than the concept', insofar as the field *is* nothing else than the tension of form. Sensation is the internal resonance or 'the contracted vibration that has become quality, variety. That is why the brain-subject is called here *soul* or *force*, since only the soul preserves by contracting that which matter dissipates, or radiates, furthers, reflects, refracts or converts' (199/211). Thus, there will be as many constituent souls as there are centres of sensation; as many 'micro-brains' as there are primary forces capable of contracting their elements by making them resonate on the plane of composition – the bearer of all varieties and things in the universe, animate and inanimate. To restrict sensation to organized living beings would be to forget that becoming is not the becoming of individualized being, but rather *the individuating becoming of being* (Simondon); it would be to confuse the empirical subject with the *transcendental physical subject*, which is the result of a prehension that the subject incorporates and which it did not pre-exist as an individuated being (Whitehead); finally, it would be to understand sensation as an element extracted from the derived action-reaction chain, whilst 'contraction is not an action, but a pure passion, a contemplation that preserves the before in the after' (199/212) and fills up its sensation of itself 'by filling itself with what it contemplates' (200/212).

In-dividuation, in-formation, *enjoyment* and *self-enjoyment* through which beings affect themselves by creating themselves, a mystery of passion and continued creation – sensation is an *inject*. That explains why, drawing as it does upon Neo-Platonism for the material conditions of an *ungrounding* [*effondement*] *of Platonism*,[31] the whole of the empiricist tradition is speculative – a speculative materialism. For 'these are not Ideas that we contemplate through concepts but the elements of matter that we contemplate through sensation. The plant contemplates by contracting the elements from which it originates – light, carbon and the salts – and it fills itself with colours and odours that *in each case* qualify its variety, its composition: it is sensation in itself' (200/212).

Contemplation means the sensible photosynthesis of what infinitizes itself between the cosmic and the elementary. This amounts to positing that sensation, through an 'identity without a functionary subject',[32] im-plicates Thought *qua* sensible

[31] I tried to set out the conditions of enunciation and ramifications of this Deleuzian theme in 'La pharmacie, Platon et le simulacre. Ontologie et logographie', in *Nos Grecs et leurs modernes*, ed. Barbara Cassin (Paris: Seuil, 1992), pp. 211–31; translated as 'Ontology and Logography: The Pharmacy, Plato and the Simulacrum' in *Between Deleuze & Derrida*, ed. Paul Patton and John Protevi (London: Continuum, 2003), pp. 84–97. On the relations between neo-Platonism and Platonism allow me to refer to my *Capital Times*, ch. 2.

[32] Alain de Libera uses this phrase in his *Introduction à la mystique rhenane* (Paris: O.E.I.L., 1984), p. 447. It is worth recalling that the author analyses the discovery of 'authentic' neo-Platonism by the 'Rhineans' (with the translation of Proclus's *Elements of Theology* by William of Moerbeke) in terms of becoming conscious of the autonomy of thought, 'when the idea of a necessary complementarity between the philosophy of the intellect and the philosophy of nature within the same theory of the One and the universe lay claim to multiple legacies which had, until that point, either crushed or dispersed it'. *Philosophy, finally* – as de Libera exclaims. This is because the inaugural gesture of Rhinean mysticism is strictly ontological, once 'the false community of logical analogy is [. . .] founded on a real communication, on the very univocity of the communication of the divine being in the world of forms and of concepts of forms' (p. 129). This makes possible the Eckhartian theory of the trans-personal unity of (the) being in which 'God must absolutely become me, and I become absolutely God, so totally one that this "He" and this "me" become one "is" [. . .]', see Sermon 83, from the French translation by J. Ancelet-Hustache, vol. 3 (Paris, 1974–1979), p. 152–3. This movement is completed in Berthold of Moosburg, with whom the theology of assimilation makes way for the primordial *unitio*.

process, manner of being, event of the Universe. To think sensation as the universal passion of thought.

It remains to be seen what is determined here with respect to the *'I feel'* [*je sens*] *of the brain as art* in its effects on the *'I conceive' of the brain as philosophy* – as well as in the play of relations that is established with the *eject of the 'I function' of the brain as science*.

Which is what we originally intended by the expression *onto-ethology*.

What becomes of art when it is regarded from the perspective of a vitalist ontology of the sensible? There is only one possible answer: the essence of art will be less that of rendering visible the unseen or the invisible as it intersects a seeing visibility [*visibilité voyante*] . . . than of *rendering Life sensible* in its 'zones of indeterminacy'. Sensation surges forth from out of the dark depths of an enveloping animality (to use a fine phrase coined by Badiou in an article to which we shall return), perpetually out of phase and *infinitely* relating its living genesis – its genesis as affect – to the aesthetic epigenesis of the work of art. This is something like the 'savage' version of a transcendental aesthetics whose *prerequisite* would be furnished by the sensible idea of an ideal indiscernibility between art and life. As Deleuze and Guattari write: 'Life alone creates such zones where living beings whirl around, and only art can reach and penetrate them in its enterprise of *co-creation*' (164/173, my emphasis). According to a more organic and less 'dissolute' perspective (without making 'the power of a depth able to dissolve forms' too sensible), Ruyer claimed that the artist is less the father of his own work, than its twin.[33] This formula applies to our question on three levels:

Firstly, inasmuch as the work of art extracts from the representative data of objective perceptions and subjective affections a composite or a *bloc of sensations*, forming a purely intensive *being* [*être*] capable of conserving itself to the extent that it exceeds every lived experience and does not refer to any object.

---

[33] Raymond Ruyer, *Éléments de psycho-biologie*, p. 50 ('The aesthetic creation of the organism').

Ceasing to be representative, sensation becomes real 'in itself'. Art is never a question of *mimesis*, but rather of *aisthesis*: 'self-position of the created' in the guise of the *monument* – Combray, *so that it stands alone*, as Whitehead remarked.

Secondly, art has no goal besides that of bringing to light unknown percepts and affects. Percepts and affects celebrate the event of an unprecedented coupling of forces in the joint *becoming sensible* of the 'witness', the author and the aesthetic figures he or she has put to work: 'making sensible the insensible forces that populate the world, affect us and make us become' (172/182), becoming-other, non-human becomings of man merging into the non-human landscapes of nature. Cézanne, revealing 'the base of inhuman nature upon which man has installed himself'.[34]

Finally, we reach the primary matter of the work, that which makes it appear as an *energetics* of being, a dimension of being 'which re-creates everywhere the primitive swamps of life' (164/174), 'sensation is not realised in the material without the material passing completely into the sensation, into the percept or affect. All the material becomes expressive' (157/166–7) by freeing both itself and the figures of art from an apparent transcendence, that of the Author. This process is conveyed in an exemplary manner by the emergence of a material density irreducible to all formal depth (183–4/193–5). This means that sensation appears for what it *is*: vibration, wave of forces or chaosmic fold, rhythm, scansion of a vital power that dissolves forms, plunges into chaos, opens onto the cosmos.[35] A non-organic power animates the aesthetic cosmogenesis of the possible together with the artistic heterogenesis of consciousness – of consciousness as 'the product of art in its lowliest form. [. . .]

[34] ['Cezanne's Doubt' in Maurice Merleau-Ponty, *The Merleau-Ponty Aesthetics Reader: Philosophy and Painting*, ed. Galen A. Johnson (Evanston, IL: Northwestern University Press, 1993), p. 66.]

[35] On the relationship between sensation and rhythm, see Gilles Deleuze, *Francis Bacon. Logique de la sensation* (Paris: Éd. De la Différence, 1981), pp. 28–33, especially the references to Maldiney. Taking his lead from Benveniste's *La notion de rythme dans son expression linguistique*, Jacques Garelli develops a poetics of rhythm as 'preindividual movement' and 'proto-temporal order' (*Rythmes et mondes*, pp. 422–40).

In a sense art is a morbid overgrowth of functions which lie deep in nature.'[36]

There is more than enough material here for a further debate with phenomenology. Except it is now a question of the becoming aesthetic of a phenomenology which has been instituted as the phenomenology *of* art so as to attain, in sensation-*aisthesis*, 'perceptual faith', Husserl's *Urdoxa* or *Urglaube*, as well as the 'chiasmus of the sensible' incarnated *in* the 'body proper': the world turns inside out, becomes seeing-visible [*voyant-visible*], a sensible squared [*à la deuxième puissance*] that leads the gaze to discover, 'beneath strictly speaking real perceptions', as Merleau-Ponty elucidates, the fleshy essence of the thing. Thus it is as the *expression of the body-of-man perceiving* (itself) that all painting paints the birth of things, the coming to self of the visible, 'illustrating and amplifying the metaphysical structure of our flesh'.[37] Flesh of the world and flesh of the body, constituting the being of sensation in that experience, which we ourselves are, of the ideal reversibility of the sensing and the sensed, of inside and outside – that would be the origin of art. Incarnating the narcissistic principle of being, the flesh would be the last notion of a metaphysics of vision – the *Urpräsentierbarkeit* in person, the visibility of the invisible.[38] Deleuze and Guattari counter these philosophical developments with the following blunt rejection: 'A universe-cosmos is not flesh' (171/180).

[36] Whitehead, *Adventures of Ideas*, p. 271.

[37] Maurice Merleau-Ponty, 'Eye and Mind' in *The Merleau-Ponty Aesthetics Reader*, p. 129.

[38] See Merleau-Ponty, *Résumés de cours* (Paris: Gallimard, 1968), pp. 177–8: 'the body proper is a sensible and it is the "sensing" [*le sentant*], it is seen and it sees, it is touched and it touches and, in its second aspect, it possesses a side which is inaccessible to others and is accessible solely to its owner. The body proper envelops a philosophy of the flesh as visibility of the invisible' (1959–60). Translated as *Themes from the Lectures at the Collège de France, 1952–1960*, trans. John O'Neill (Evanston, IL: Northwestern University Press, 1970) [translation modified]. [For a similar passage see also 'Nature and Logos: The Human Body', in *In Praise of Philosophy and Other Essays* (Evanston, IL: Northwestern University Press, 1970), p. 197.] One could also refer to the celebrated pages of the *Phenomenology of Perception*, trans. Colin Smith (London: Routledge, 2002), pp. 308–11, where Merleau-Ponty uncovers a 'primordial depth' beneath objectified depth.

A. *The universe-cosmos is not a world* because of the very traits of alterity and alteration that separate art from the perception without which the world could not be given to us or even be 'formed' . . . As Emmanuel Lévinas noted, even the most realist of the arts presupposes the possibility of the absence of forms – what Malevich called *the transfiguration of forms into zero* – and therefore 'the nontransmutation of exteriority into inwardness, which forms realise'; art gives rise to a feeling of *exoticism* with regard to every distinction between an inside and an outside. By celebrating 'the very event of sensation *qua* sensation, the aesthetic event', sensible quality loses its worldly and world-making property. As aesthetic, the event starts to exist *in itself* once sensation ceases to re-present to itself the material of perception, returning instead to the impersonality of the *element* of the sensible and to the non-organic life of a becoming which ignores the ontological frame of the lived body. This is evident in 'the undifferentiated blocks which Rodin's statues emerge from. Reality is posited in them in its exotic nakedness as a worldless reality [. . .]. The discovery of the materiality of being is not a discovery of a new quality, but of its formless production [*grouille-ment*]. Behind the luminosity of forms, by which beings already relates to our "inside", matter is the very fact of the *there is* [*il y a*]'[39] into which art plunges. There is: art.

By passing into the powers of life that support its fragile texture, the flesh lets transpire a materiality, 'which wells up [. . .] beneath the bands of crimson' [*qui monte sous les plages d'incar-nat*] (169/179). The flesh turns into a *skin* that spans genera, orders and domains; an imprint of the cosmos, a surging up of

[39] Emmanuel Lévinas, *Existence and Existents*, trans. Alphonso Lingis (The Hague: Martinus Nijhoff, 1978), pp. 53, 55, 57. For Merleau-Ponty, it is instead the *visual quale* that 'gives me, and is alone in doing so, the presence of what is not me, of what *is* simply and fully. It does so because, as a texture, it is the concretion of a universal visibility, of one sole Space that separates and reunites, *that sustains every cohesion*' ('Eye and Mind', p. 147, my emphasis). Rodin's 'silent science' will consist in letting pass into the work 'the forms of things "whose seal has not been broken"' just like '[p]ainting searches not for the outside of movement but for its secret ciphers' (p. 145). The *autofigurative* dimension of the painting will therefore puncture 'the skin of things' [Henri Michaux, quoted by Merleau-Ponty] *only in order to* 'show how the things become things, how the world becomes world' (p. 141).

the ground [*sol*], leading the painter to become the explorer of a hyperphysical world where *to see is akin to becoming imbued* with the allotropic variations of the universal force field, where to sense is to *capture, as if by surprise, the image of secret facts, of unknown stages in the formation of things.*[40] The skin is deepest . . . Or, of the philosophy of art as a general dermatology.

From the formless swarming of the aesthetic materiality of being, affirmed by Lévinas, to Dubuffet's declared savagery, a single reproach seems to rise up against the 'barbaric principle' called *flesh*: it's too tender, 'the flesh is too tender', it is merely 'the thermometer of a becoming' (169/179). Which is another way of saying that the flesh is too civilized, that it is still too close to the teleology of consciousness endorsed by the *Phenomenology of Perception*. After all, isn't that the reason why Merleau-Ponty felt the need to relate art to an identity of origin that pre-exists it: the world perceived by the lived body without objective intentionality, the primacy of perception leading to that 'strange insensibility to the pictorial affect' and to colours lamented by Michel Haar?[41] That's the reply to the Malraux of *The Voices of Silence*:

[40] Unfortunately, I can only refer here to Dubuffet's extraordinary text, *Empreintes*, April 1957, reprinted in *Prospectus et tous écrits suivants* (Paris: Gallimard, 1967), vol. II – a text that one would like to prolong in the direction of an *aesthetics of the symptom* as forwarded by Georges Didi-Huberman in the Appendix to *Devant l'image* (Paris: Minuit, 1990). [Let us note in passing that the cover of the French edition of *The Signature of the World* reproduces a 'detail' from a painting by Dubuffet belonging to the series: *Texturologies: Life Without Man I*.]

[41] Michel Haar, 'Peinture, perception, affectivité' in M. Richir and E. Tassin (eds.), *Merleau-Ponty, phénoménologie et expérience* (Grenoble: Millon, 1992), p. 117. The author notes that the only interpretation of Cézanne's colours in *The Eye and the Mind* concerns white. In the *Portrait of Vallier* the whites arranged between the colours 'have as their function to construct [*façonner*], to *extract a more general being* than being-yellow or being-green or being-blue . . .' (p. 68, my emphasis). The dimension of colour modulating things in instability will then be able to 'make the spectacle-form crack' (pp. 66–7) and *force the limits of an analysis of perception* by partially freeing it from the empiricism of the lived and the perceived (see Claude Imbert, 'Le bleu de la mer années 50', *Traverses* 4 [1992]). It remains the case that painting is still an 'objective consciousness' to the extent that *colour is the place where our brain and the universe meet* (Cézanne, quoted by Merleau-Ponty in 'Eye and Mind', p. 141). On Cézanne's painting as a *modulation of colour*, one must refer to the two studies by Lawrence Gowing, exhibition catalogue, *Watercolour and Pencil Drawings by Cézanne* (London:

it remains the case that Renoir gazed at the sea to throw back the fish and keep watch over his line . . .

B. *The body has no organs, only thresholds and levels*: a) which enter into composition with the 'patches' (171/179)[42] that provide the flesh with its armature (the sensation-house); b) which open the most tightly sealed 'house' onto a universe functioning as a potential (from territory to deterritorialization, from the finite to the infinite). Moreover, within the event of painting, the body is no longer anything but the zone of indiscernibility between the plane and the skin, the effect of delegitimation of perceptual evidence, the panic at the surface, a *histeresis* where one comes to feel the 'perpetual demand for a topological conversion of the plane as an effect of the skin'.[43] This is an effect of the 'patch' [*pan*], *pannus*: a strip of the plane that exchanges and adjusts the compound, comprising the non-human forces of the cosmos and the non-human becomings of man, such that 'the painting is therefore not just a topics [*topique*], but a dynamics and an energetics of the living'.[44] The patch forces us to rethink the surface as a skin stretched upon the symptomal night of the *there is*, *imprinting* the silent and invisible violence of a *praesens* which would thereby have evaded the general laws of being so as

Footnote 41 (*continued*)
Arts Council, 1973) and 'The Logic of Organized Sensations' (1977), now in Michael Doran (ed.), *Conversations with Cézanne* (Berkeley, CA: The University of California Press, 2001). At the intersection of all these interpretations, let us keep in mind this maxim by Cézanne: 'One should not say model, but *module*' ['*On ne devrait pas dire modeler, on devrait dire moduler*'].
   [42] [To avoid the confusion elicited by the translation of both *coupe* and *pan* as 'section' in the English text of *What is Philosophy?* and to maintain the specificity of the aesthetic reference, we have opted both here and in the epigraph to the chapter for 'patch'. This is indeed how *pan* is translated in the English text of Proust's *The Captive*, where, in the famous passage on Vermeer's 'View of Delft', the narrator speaks repeatedly of a *petit pan de mur jaune*, 'a little patch of yellow wall'. We thank Georges Didi-Huberman for pointing us toward Proust's text. The latin *pannus*, see below, translates as 'rag, patch, piece of cloth'.]
   [43] Georges Didi-Huberman, *La peinture incarnée* (Paris: Minuit, 1985), p. 37.
   [44] Didi-Huberman, p. 36. This is what led Malevich to say that 'each pictorial surface is more alive than any face stuffed with a pair of eyes and a smile' ('From Cubism and Futurism to Suprematism: The New Painterly Realism').

to auto-present itself as a *matter* extravagating upon the body, endowed with the power of a 'not yet' = *in praesentia*. (As Lévinas notes, we could thus speak of nights in full daylight [*nuits en plein jour*].) This is because the skin is the dimension implied by the 'emergence of pure sensory qualities, of sensibilia that cease to be merely functional and become expressive features' (174/183).

The skin – or the territory.

C. *'Perhaps art begins with the animal, at least with the animal that carves out a territory and constructs a house'* (174/183, my emphasis); art makes it so that matter separates itself from the matter of content to become a matter of expression – a skin and a territory, since both are needed if we are to liberate the possible which lies concealed beneath matters and forms of content. We could say it is the skin, this 'aesthetic' epigenesis *in actu*, which will permit us to *describe* the philosophical concept of territory as a torsion of the world that locally singularizes the qualitative continuity of the multiple into a being of sensation ('an outpouring of features, colours and sounds that are inseparable insofar as they become expressive' [174/184]): the territory would, in this sense, be the effect of art. Or, alternatively, we could say that art begins with the territory *qua* auto-movement of expressive qualities producing a territorialization of milieus and rhythms for which the skin functions as something like a first dimension: art opens onto the cosmic forces it both contracts and modulates. The crucial point is that from both points of view 'art does not wait for man to begin'[45]; art is the concern of a philosophy *of* nature, insofar as the latter 'combines these two living elements in every way [. . .] territory and deterritorialisation, finite melodic compounds and the great infinite plane of composition, the small and large refrain' (176/186).

To sum up, nature and art alike partake in a melodic vitalism which attains an expressionism brut with the sudden appearance of the

---

[45] *A Thousand Plateaus*, p. 394/320 ('1837: On the Refrain') [translation modified].

territory and the house; the expressiveness diffused in life 'becomes constructive and erects ritual monuments of an animal mass that celebrates qualities' (174/184). Territory is *quality caught up in the becoming which grasps it*, art brut, nature-art. Lorenz is therefore 'wrong' to want to explain territory by a phylogenetic evolution of functions because, as always already territorialized, these functions presuppose the territorializing expressiveness which produces territory and negotiates a synthesis of heterogeneous elements, thereby constituting the scenopoietic assemblage (heterogenesis). Similarly, against a certain phenomenology of animal behaviour, we will never comprehend the indistinction of body and environment on the basis of the *ring* of capture from which the animal *poor in world* (*weltarm*) would have no means of distinguishing itself ('behavioural capture'[46]); rather, we should start out from the colour-becomings and sound-becomings, the rhythms and counterpoints set into a *refrain* by the animal in the movement of territorialization.

These are the *prerequisites* for a superior ethology: to think in terms of becoming rather than evolution, of expressive qualities rather than functions, of assemblages rather than behaviours.

Heterogenesis contra phylogenesis, with naturing nature as a processual paradigm, a new aesthetic paradigm implying the experimental gesture of a contingent reason – a geographical and ethological instead of a historical reason – such that the life of the world it describes or 'follows' can include description itself as *the inside of the outside*, 'when the outside hollows itself out and lures interiority . . .'[47]

I propose to call onto-ethology the establishment of a plane of

---

[46] I am thinking here principally of the analysis of animality that Heidegger gave in his 1929–30 course entitled *Grundbegriffe der Metaphysik*, *Gesamtausgabe*, vols. 29–30 (Klosterman: Frankfurt-am-Main, 1983), pp. 295–396; *The Fundamental Concepts of Metaphysics: World, Finitude, Solitude*, trans. William McNeill and Nicholas Walker (Bloomington: Indiana University Press, 2001). Marc Richir offers a particularly fine commentary on this text in his *Phénoménologie et institution symbolique* (Grenoble: Millon, 1988), pp. 223–85. Richir adroitly highlights the shared view of Heidegger and Lorenz before dissociating himself from it from the perspective of a grasp of the 'phenomenological' and of 'eidetic variation' in the animal.

[47] [Blanchot, quoted in Gilles Deleuze, *Foucault* (Paris: Minuit, 1986), p. 93.]

immanence such that, *becoming and multiplicity being one and the same, becoming no longer has a subject distinct from itself* and carries thinking along with it as the heterogenesis of nature: a plane of nature. It is the plane of nature that provides the 'there' wherein to 'go in order to search would be to create' (197/209) (the brain): a becoming conceptual of philosophy which determines mental objects as real beings, as the production and constitution of things themselves in the mind; a becoming sensible of art which composes beings of sensation exceeding all lived experience, enriched as they are by all the fields of the possible; a becoming nature of a referred chaos which science cannot coordinate without drawing on a chaotic potential that compels it to confront all sorts of fluctuations and bifurcations. A triple becoming of thought as creation carving itself out on a background of 'chaosmosis'; a triple deterritorialization of the system of opinion and its three orthodoxies: communication (of propositions), unification (of the true), recognition (of lived experience [*vécu*]).

Three ways of saying that *What is Philosophy?* was written from the *philosophical* point of view of a thought thinking itself in the struggle against *doxa*, that it sought to raise the question of philosophy in its relations to science and art in order to show 'the basis of a relationship between science and philosophy, science and art, and philosophy and art' (126/132): Nature-Art. Moreover, it wanted to discover the forces under whose influence nature is thrice made immanent: I conceive, I feel, I function . . . Modifying ever so slightly Macherey's elegant formula: Deleuze in Spinoza is also Spinoza in Deleuze-Guattari.

('A sort of philosophy of Nature, now that any distinction between nature and artifice is becoming blurred' is how Deleuze announced the reprise of his collaboration with Guattari.[48])

Our formula will only make sense once the internal relations between the most contemporary science and this problematic have been examined with greater precision.

We have seen that the constitution of a system of reference

---

[48] Gilles Deleuze, *Pourparlers* (Paris: Minuit, 1990), p. 212; *Negotiations*, trans. Martin Joughin (New York: Columbia University Press, 1994), p. 155.

capable of coordinating the slowing down of matter and trans-
lating its functional actualization into equations is conditioned
by the realization of experiments that make 'partial observers'
appear in the neighbourhood of singularities, observers whose
function is *to put the functives to the test of the sensible*. To be
more precise: 'partial observers' *construct* the point of view on
the basis of which the sensible truth of a variation extracted from
the instability and complexity of elementary particles can be
affirmed *in things themselves*. But what then is a singularity, if
not these perceptions and affections which 'give meaning'
[*donnent sens*] to functives by endowing them with a 'sensibility'?
It is these sensible forces, these veritable *scientific sensibilia*,
which forbid the separation of a state of affairs from the potential through which it operates . . . For the universe itself has a
history in becoming and a *life*. We cannot avoid quoting
Prigogine and Stengers here: 'Use of the term "sensibility" in this
context does not imply an anthropomorphic projection, but
rather signifies an *enrichment of the notion of causality*. [. . .] The
notion of "sensibility" joins together what physicists are in the
habit of separating: the definition of a system and its activity.'[49]

The consequences of such a stance are considerable, since the
logicization in abstracto of the function will be opposed, in
Deleuze and Guattari, by the *animation in concreto* of the functives. The 'crisis of foundations' can now be regarded as nothing
but the symptom of the failure of an ambition: that of discovering, in the fantasy of a knowledge severed from its roots, the
transparency of a thoroughly rational world. This so-called
crisis of foundations is answered by the reaffirmation of the privilege of the living, of a world alive from top to bottom, where the
pressure of the virtual ceaselessly expresses the 'lived experience'
of things, a world where all is force, interaction and prehension,
affection and perception, sensibility and sensibility to – composition of forces and affects.

Thus one can no longer simply define a body by its form and
its functions, lineage or filiation – Lorenz will be proven wrong,
for in the end animism 'is not so far removed from biological

[49] Prigogine and Stengers, *Entre le temps et l'éternité*, p. 60.

science as it is said to be' (124/130), if in these domains too there is no total observer capable of integrating the future and the past in the unveiled enigma of phylogenetic adaptation.

As Prigogine and Stengers masterfully showed in their *Order Out of Chaos*, that is also why Darwinian theory currently finds itself as the model for the sciences, since it satisfies the three minimal requirements without which it will henceforth be impossible to think the universe: irreversibility, the event and new coherencies[50] that tend to establish a direct communication between the microphysical and the cosmic.

This opens up the prospect of a universal vitalism which relaunches science in its struggle against 'properly scientific opinion' and *determines the point of view from which science and philosophy enter into a relationship*, that of a *molecular Darwinism* taking Spinoza 'by the middle' *in the anexact and yet absolutely rigorous part of his thought.*[51]

What we have here is an *intra-philosophical* perspective that allows us to grasp the relations of forces [*rapports de forces*] constitutive of contemporary science, as well as the forces that constitute the cosmos in accordance with a principle which is no longer that of sufficient reason but rather one of resonance and correspondence. To the relationships of speed and slowness of *non-formed elements* that compose and decompose 'bodies', there now correspond the intensities of an *anonymous force* affecting them at each and every instant[52] and expressed by partial observers. 'Nothing but affects and local movements, differential speeds' bring science infinitely closer to the very chaos it intended to organize. The question of science thus turns

[50] Prigogine and Stengers, pp. 45–8 and 180: 'The articulation between the physico-chemical and biology will not pass by a physicalisation of life, but by a historicisation of the physico-chemical, by the discovery of the possibilities of the discovery of the physico-chemical history of matter.' On the importance of Darwinism for Deleuze and Guattari, see *A Thousand Plateaus*, pp. 47–50.

[51] See Deleuze, *Negotiations*, pp. 44–5/29 on the two sorts of scientific notions: on the one hand, 'notions that are exact in nature, quantitative, defined by equations', and on the other notions that are 'essentially anexact yet completely rigorous', because their rigour escapes the criterion of exactitude. The two types are ceaselessly and concretely mixing with each other.

[52] See Deleuze, *Spinoza: Practical Philosophy*, pp. 171–2/127–8, for definitions of the longitude and latitude of a body.

into that of becoming, in other words, 'of elements and particles, which do not arrive fast enough to effect a passage, a becoming or jump on the same plane of pure immanence [. . .]. A fixed plane of life upon which everything stirs, slows down or accelerates. A single abstract Animal for all the assemblages that effectuate it'.[53]

Science thus threatens to become 'Spinozist' and 'ethological', driven by this *ethos* which refers the translation of affects into energetic relationships to Nature-Art's plane of composition. It is no longer the Animal *or* the Number – as Badiou would have it[54] – since science must take into account the Nature *of* the Animal that forces it to accompany this 'sinuous, *reptilian* movement' determined by the *chaoid variables* which interfere with the co-ordinating system for information about initial conditions. Placed under the sign of the creation of new coherencies, this movement opens up the sciences to the problem of becoming and to the question of the emergence of the new. Contradicting the Bergsonian diagnosis, it asserts the *actuality* of a science of the becomings of matter.

It is up to such a non-Galilean science to 'make evident the chaos into which the brain itself, as subject of knowledge, plunges' (203/215–6), emerging in the midst of uncertain connections and following the rhizomatic figures that give rise to individuations and bifurcations. Beyond cognitivism therefore – because as Milner correctly argues 'cognitivism, as a Galilean science of the understanding, encounters exactly the same problems as the Galilean sciences of nature'.[55] A constant interchange must be established between contemporary images of thought and the current state of the sciences of the brain (as an 'uncertain nervous system'). Accordingly, the question becomes that of an ethology of thought capable of following the uncharted furrows that every new creation (of concepts, functions or sensations) traces in the brain: new connections, new pathways, new synapses . . . We are faced here with something like a *material image* that the biology of the brain discovers with

[53] *A Thousand Plateaus*, pp. 318, 312/260, 255 [translation modified].
[54] 'Gilles Deleuze, *The Fold: Leibniz and the Baroque*', p. 55.
[55] Milner, p. 205.

its own means[56] and which is not without bearing on the onto-ethological nature of the concept.

Picking things up from the beginning, a beginning that could not be specified until the end: what is a concept, if not an intensive *rhizome* in a state of survey with regard to its components; a rhizome that thereby becomes equivalent to the brain, one of whose points of view it constitutes? As a point of view on the brain *qua* point of view on the concept, the concept of the concept accompanies, from the opening pages of *What is Philosophy?* onward, the path of a rhizomorphic narration capable of describing the conceptual heterogenesis of the principle of multiplicity. The concept of the concept is the concept that makes it possible to *perceive* the modality of its own apparition, in the description of its operations and of its internal organization as a processual multiplicity. (In this sense, to create concepts is to make every concept into the concept of its own concept: the concept as creation, as singular, non-universal process: self-positing of the concept. Has anyone noticed that all of Deleuze and Guattari's 'great' concepts are *concepts of the concept*?) A pragmatics of the concept coming under a logic of multiplicities – this is philosophy as the becoming autochthonous of thought, the regional thinking of becoming 'constructed locally, going from one point to the next'.[57]

There follows a triple genesis of the concept: as an open, consistent and intensive multiplicity. *An open multiplicity*: 'every concept has components that may, in turn, be grasped as concepts [. . .]. Concepts, therefore, extend to infinity' (24–5/19). *A consistent multiplicity*: 'what is distinctive about the concept is that it renders components inseparable *within itself*: distinct, heterogeneous and yet not separable, that is the status of components' (25/19). This is the *ethological* status of the concept in its position as an assemblage relative to components which do not delimit an ideal territory on the plane without, by the same token, prolonging themselves in the lines of deterritorialization that refer each

---

[56] *Negotiations*, p. 204/149; *Cinema 2: The Time-Image*, p. 271/212, it is also the case that our relationship with the brain will have first changed, 'obscurely guiding science'.

[57] *Negotiations*, p. 204/147.

concept to other concepts . . . *An intensive multiplicity* 'in a state of *survey* in relation to its components, endlessly traversing them according to an order without distance [. . .] it is a refrain, an opus with its number' (26/20–1). The ethological refrain of the concept, tracing its territory (the contour of its components) according to a necessarily finite movement, is coupled here to an *ontological* refrain that corresponds to the *really absolute unity* produced at infinite speed by the non-dimensional or '*intensional*' survey of its components. Without this 'metaphysical' transversal of the field of a concept, the concept would be nothing but an assemblage of bits and pieces, a 'for itself' without an 'in itself', subjected to an ordering procedure in accordance with a pre-established meaning, a meaning relative to a point of view external to itself. Survey and infinite speed are machinic, not metaphorical, notions; they assert the auto-objective act that conditions the reality of every intensive multiplicity: being 'at the source of all linkages, rather than the result of linkages and assemblages of parts'. This is because the concept, like the brain *or being*, 'consists of the "montage" (in the active sense of the word) of linkages and not of functioning *according to* a montage (in the passive sense)'[58]; this is *the concept as a real being*, a fold of the brain folding in on itself, micro-brain. Or, to employ a different vocabulary: the concept is a '*conceptional*' being (*ens conceptionale*), a *thought-being*; it is being and thought simultaneously: 'thought of being *and* being of thought. The thought-being does not know itself simply as being but as thought-of-being; but, at the same time, it is a being only as recognition of thought [. . .]. The thought-being or known being is being *qua this* being [. . .] and it is a thought-being to the extent that it is nothing but the activity of knowing'.[59] Intellect, the agent

---

[58] Ruyer, *Néo-finalisme*, p. 124. For his part, Guattari writes 'The entity is modulation of consistency, rhythm of assembly and disassembly', *Cartographies schizo-analytiques*, p. 138.

[59] Alain de Libera, *Introduction à la mystique rhénane*, pp. 210–214. We owe to Thierry of Freiberg, in his *De Visione Beatifica*, the introduction of the notion of *ens conceptionale*. See B. Mojsisch, 'Sein als Bewußt-Sein', in *Von Meister Dietrich zu Meister Eckhart*, ed. K. Flasch (Hamburg, 1984); and, in the same volume, M.R. Pagnoni-Sturlese, 'Filosofia della natura e filosofia dell'intelletto in Teodorico de Freiberg e Bertoldo de Moosburg', for the Proclusian bases of this conception.

of the possible intellect and the possibility of the agent intellect: *Bewußtsein*. Thus the concept is flux, and it is flux as the noetic form of action and the ontological action of form. As *Bewußt-Sein*, the concept passes through the introduction of a kind of *biology of intellectual action*. Fichte – who Deleuze and Guattari quote (195/207) – is 'Rhinean' when he introduces the concept of *Tathandlung* (state of action) to posit, at the foundation of his *Science of Knowledge*, 'not a being, but a life'[60]; that is, a *genesis* manifesting, on the basis of the originary indistinction of intuition and concept, the materialization of form as content ('form become the form of form itself *qua* its content'[61]). It matters little here that the genesis of the concept as 'living and active thing which engenders insights from (*aus*) and through itself, and which the philosopher merely contemplates',[62] partakes in the originary reflection of a pure 'I' [*Moi*] – since it is still the concept which places it on a plane of immanence such that *intuition becomes intellectual at the same time as the concept becomes concrete.*[63]

[60] J. G. Fichte, *Second Introduction to the Science of Knowledge* (*S. W.*, I, p. 465) 'Not a being . . .' because in that case the *logical* determination of the concept by the predicate of the real being would be valid. The principle 'of the difference between logic, as a purely formal science, and real philosophy, or metaphysics' would then disappear (*S. W.*, I, pp. 496). 'Second Introduction to the Science of Knowledge', in *Fichte: The Science of Knowledge*, ed. and trans. Peter Heath and John Lachs (Cambridge: Cambridge University Press, 1982 [1970]), pp. 40, 67. [Translation modified, Heath and Lachs render this as 'not a matter of existence, but of life'.]

[61] Fichte, *On the Concept of the Science of Knowledge or of what is called Philosophy* (*S. W.*, I, p. 67). On *Tathandlung* as *genesis*, see *Theory of Knowledge, 1804 Exposition* (*Nachgelassene Werke*, I, p. 194).

[62] Fichte, *Second Introduction* (*S. W.*, I, p. 454); English translation, p. 30. What the *Science of Knowledge* takes as the object of its reflection is 'not a lifeless concept, passively exposed to its inquiry merely, of which it makes something only by its own thought, but . . .'.

[63] See Jacques Vuillemin, *L'héritage kantien et la révolution copernicienne* (Paris: PUF, 1954), p. 75. Delbos remarks with great acumen that in Fichte 'Intelligence is an acting, *ein Thun*, and nothing more; it should not even be called an active subject, *ein Thätiges*, because such an expression would make one think of something subsisting, whose activity would be a property', see Victor Delbos, *De Kant aux postkantiens*, 2nd ed. (Paris: Aubier, 1992). Such a property would refer immanence to . . . (but see the (post-)analytical note above for an approach that we consider to be more 'historiographical').

84 *The Signature of the World*

To conclude, we can say that the relativity and absoluteness of the concept, as both territory and absolute volume (the 'earth' of the concept), are like its ethology and ontology, united by constructivism. It is as if the ontological intension of the concept were that of a 'superior ethology' putting thought into direct relationship with the earth, on a celestial line of flight which can inscribe itself at the bottom of the sea. 'The Deterritorialised *par excellence*': the Earth is the concept of the concept of concept, the Homeland [*le Natal*] of the philosopher. Philosophy as a *noomadology*[64] – what Guattari called an ecology of the virtual.

Fortified by this conceptual vitalism, thought acquires a pedagogy of the concept that *starts to function in the manner of a natural history*. To write the natural history of the concept, but also of each concept in itself and in relation to others, like one produces the concept of a bird, not 'in its genus or species but in the composition of its postures, colours and songs' (25/20). It is in this sense that Deleuze and Guattari aim to restore to the concept its evental power [*puissance d'événement*], a power that must befall the thought that creates it in order to act directly upon the brain, displacing the limit between the concrete and the abstract, the sensible and the intelligible; that is, engendering the *interference* – on a background of non-dialectical disparity – of art, science and philosophy.

Thought as heterogenesis, or the bird as event: Spinoza, the firebird of philosophy.

Since by borrowing the autochthonous language of that of which *and those of whom* one speaks, *animealiter*, 'thought itself is sometimes closer to a dying animal than to the living man, even a democrat' (103/108).[65]

Paris, Linkebeek, Pino Marine, Rio de Janeiro, January–October
1992
Translated by Eliot Ross Albert with Alberto Toscano

[64] [The author is here taking his cue from the discussion in Deleuze and Guattari's *A Thousand Plateaus* of the 'noosphere' and playing on the relationship between *nôos* and *noûs*, whose etymology does not simply connote 'intellectual' but also 'dynamic and emotional'. See R.B. Onians, *The Origins of European Thought about the Body, the Mind, the Soul, the World, Time and Fate* (Cambridge: Cambridge University Press, 1951), p. 83.]

[65] [Translation modified.]

Appendix I   Deleuze's Virtual Philosophy*

In memoriam

Let's not ask what principles are, but what they do.

Gilles Deleuze

I would like here, briefly, to assemble and disassemble a paradox that every reader of Gilles Deleuze, whether amateur or seasoned scholar, will have come across in one way or another. For though it is undeniable that the monographs on Hume, Bergson, Nietzsche, Kant and Spinoza offer a veritable genesis of Deleuzian thought, it is no less true that the relation of *doubling* entertained by Deleuze with regard to the history of philosophy[1] ends up causing trouble, not for the philosophical identity of his thought (a 'philosophy of difference', according to the more generic definition; or, more rigorously, a 'philosophy of the event'), *but with respect to the practice and reality of this philosophy, which in the final analysis has no other*

---

* This is a revised version of the closing address at the memorial day organized by the *Colégio Internacional de Estudos Filosoficos Transdisciplinares*, December 5, 1995 in Rio de Janeiro (Centro Cultural Banco do Brasil), under the title 'Gilles Deleuze: uma vida filosofica'. [This essay was originally published as *Deleuze philosophie virtuelle* (Paris: Synthélabo, 1996).]
    [1] See the frequently cited Preface to *Difference and Repetition*: 'In the history of philosophy, a commentary should act as a veritable double and bear the maximal modification appropriate to a double', p. 4/xxi.]

question than that of thought and of the images of thought that motivate it.

It is under the sign of this paradox and this difficulty that I interpret Roberto Machado's conclusion in a book entitled *Deleuze e a filosofia*: 'Deleuzian philosophy is less the announcement of a new thought than a sum of thoughts, which it relates in order to express, at one level or another, difference.'[2] You can already imagine, by transparency and difference, what will be the question that I would at the very least like to raise this evening: under what conditions is it possible to affirm that the *free indirect discourse* enlisted by Deleuze to constitute the differential space of his oeuvre – 'a wall of loose stones, uncemented stones, where every element has a value in itself but also in relation to the others' or 'an infinite patchwork with multiple joinings' ('Bartleby; or, The formula')[3] – is the creator of a new thought and a new image of thought: *Deleuzism*?

In my view, there are two possible options.

The first, of a theoretical nature, consists in installing oneself on the plane defined extensively by *A Thousand Plateaus* and intensively by *What is Philosophy?*, taking up a position overhanging the monographs. But in the end, why should one strive to reconstitute the equation with all the terms it implies if the result clearly shows that we are dealing with a qualitative and continuous multiplicity – and not with a sum of thoughts whose common measure would be provided by the number of elements it contains? I already experienced this 'Bergsonian' predicament in the writing of *The Signature of the World*.

The second option, which we could call practical or empirical, consists in grasping in the philosophical monographs what Deleuze selects and makes return *as pure intensive states of the anonymous force of thought* only in order to affirm *the transmutation of philosophy as such*. When, in the name of anarchic difference, philosophy undertakes the exclusion of all the

---

[2] Roberto Machado, *Deleuze e a filosofia* (Rio de Janeiro: Graal, 1990), p. 225.

[3] [*Essays Critical and Clinical*, trans. Daniel W. Smith and Michael A. Greco (London: Verso, 1998), p. 86.]

transcendent principles it encountered in its history, whenever it needed to adapt itself to the Forms of God, the World and the I (centre, sphere and circle: 'the triple condition for not being able to think the event'[4]); when philosophy affirms immanence as the only condition allowing it to re-create its concepts as 'the things themselves, but things in a wild and free state, beyond "anthropological predicates."'[5]

Already at this level, what is 'new' in Deleuze would be the fact that the speculative radicality of his ontology determines, on this line devoid of contour (this *line of flight*), the possibility of a *finally* revolutionary philosophical materialism. An Ideal-materialism of the pure event, indefinitely multiple and singularly universal, according to these words of Foucault which apply perfectly to the philosophies put-into-becoming by Deleuze? Thought-Event or, via Nietzsche and Bergson finally reunited, the 'creation' of thought proceeding by *virtualization*. Everything points to the conclusion that one could qualify in this manner the movement of 'desubstantialization' and 'problematization' of the history of philosophy operated by Deleuze under the name of *deterritorialization*; if virtualization, as Pierre Lévy shows, consists above all in transforming 'the initial actuality into a particular case of a more general problematic, upon which the ontological emphasis is then placed. In so doing, virtualisation makes fluid the instituted distinctions, augments the degrees of freedom, hollows out a moving void' . . . Everything happens as if Deleuzian deterritorialization raised the 'authors' under consideration to the power of *fluctuating evental nodes that interface and envelop one another reciprocally* on one and the same plane of immanence.[6] So many authors, so many assemblages capable of being actualized in the

---

[4] Michel Foucault, 'Theatrum Philosophicum' (1970), trans. Daniel F. Brouchard and Sherry Simon, in *Aesthetics, Method, Epistemology: The Essential Works of Foucault, 1954–1984, Volume 2*, ed. James D. Faubion (London: Allen Lane/Penguin, 1998), pp. 343–68.

[5] *Difference and Repetition*, p. 3/xxi, translation modified.

[6] Virtualization is not derealization but deterritorialization, see Pierre Lévy, *Qu'est-ce que le virtuel?* (Paris: La Découverte, 1995), Chapters 1 and 9. For a Deleuze-inspired elaboration of the question of the virtual image, see Jean-Clet Martin, *L'image virtuelle* (Paris: Kimé, 1998). Whilst I was revising the final version of this text, Jean-Luc Nancy sent me his contribution to Paul Patton's

most diverse figures and questions: of philosophy as the art of assemblages on which 'principles' depend (and not the other way around . . .), a problematizing creation coinciding with the emergence of the *new* whose only subject is the virtual – a virtual whose actual is in turn nothing but a complement or product.

(This clarification of the question of the new by the notion of the virtual is corroborated by a posthumous text entitled 'The Actual and the Virtual', published in appendix to the second edition of Gilles Deleuze and Claire Parnet's *Dialogues*.)

By opting for this second method, in which it is less a matter of potentializing philosophies (by formalizing them) than of virtualizing them (and actualizing them) according to a 'perpetual exchange between the virtual and the actual' *which defines the plane of immanence as such*, one will necessarily have to start, for reasons that are not simply chronological, from Deleuze's encounter with empiricism. Like a writer of science-fiction, doesn't the empiricist precisely treat the concept 'as object of an encounter, as a here-and-now, or rather as an *Erewhon* from which emerge inexhaustibly ever new, differently distributed "heres" and "nows"' – as Deleuze writes in the aforementioned preface?[7] The Empiricist, or the great Experimenter.

* * *

Empiricism and Subjectivity: An Essay on Hume's Theory of Human Nature, published in 1953 (the 'Hume-assemblage', as we will later read), effectively kicks off Deleuze's research through what he discovers in empiricism: a *philosophy of experience* which

Footnote 6 (*continued*)
Deleuze: A Critical Reader (London: Blackwell, 1996), 'The Deleuzian Fold of Thought'. In it, I was struck to find the following statement: 'The philosophy of Gilles Deleuze is a *virtual* philosophy, in the sense that this word is used today . . .'. Later, I was to discover, through the kindness of Claire Parnet, whom I take the opportunity to thank here, Deleuze's then unpublished text on 'The Actual and the Virtual' to which I allude below – not without finding Lévy's work cited in one of its few footnotes . . .
[7] *Difference and Repetition*, p. 3/xx.

is immediately equivalent – in the same movement and by the immanent point of view at play within it (that of associationism) – to a *critique of the metaphysics of consciousness and the philosophies of the object* (phenomenology and logical formalism included) *qua critique of representation*. This is because 'representations *cannot* present the relations' through which the subject constitutes itself in a datum which is none other than the flux of the sensible, as the ensemble of perceptions irreducible to a state of affairs and as a conjunction of relations external to their terms. Thus, 'if we call "experience" the collection of distinct perceptions, we must recognise the fact that relations do not derive from experience; they are the effect of principles of association [. . .] which, within experience, constitute a subject capable of moving beyond experience'. Thus, it is in a world of exteriority – 'a world in which thought itself exists in a fundamental relationship with the Outside',[8] as Deleuze will write in his article 'Hume' some twenty years later – a world which does not ignore a certain 'transcendental' character of sensibility, that being equals appearance for a subjectivity whose essence is practical . . . Neither theoretical (in a position of foundation or of *representative*) nor psychological (in a situation of *represented* interiority), this subjectivity is defined in and by a movement of *subjectivation* whose assemblage of beliefs and passions, freed from all transcendence (of the subject as well as the object), adjusts immanence to becoming in a continuum of intensities which composes the intensive flux of the stream of consciousness and refers back to the intensity of the idea in the stream of thought.[9]

[8] ['Hume' in *Pure Immanence: Essays on A Life*, trans. Anne Boyman (New York: Zone Books, 2001), p. 38.]

[9] We must note the importance of the Hume-James *concatenation*, characteristic of Deleuzian 'radical empiricism' (the expression was coined by James), for the critique of the Husserlian transcendental Ego, together with the frequent reference to Sartre's *The Transcendence of the Ego*. In the last text published during his lifetime, 'Immanence: A Life . . .' (originally published in *Philosophie* 47, 1995, now translated in English in *Pure Immanence: Essays on A Life*, pp. 25–33), Deleuze himself relates Sartre and James from this point of view (and cites in a note David Lapoujade's article – whose tone is quite Deleuzian – 'Le flux intensif de la conscience de William James', *Philosophie* 46, 1995); on Deleuze's empiricism see Xavier Papaïs's article 'Puissances de l'artifice', published in the special issue on Deleuze of *Philosophie*, 47, pp. 85–92.

By having thus confronted the paradox of relations, instead of reducing them to the form of interiority that characterizes the judgement of attribution, and by thus exploring the field of the *empirical* (this apparently fictive world which is in fact our own . . .), always starting from very concrete situations, empiricist philosophy lets itself be conceived as a 'vital protest against principles' (*Dialogues*, with Claire Parnet), alternating the exercise of fictions and the practice of artifice. A kind of pop philosophy *avant la lettre*, sealing the 'great conversion of theory into practice' and transforming theory into *inquiry*.

Proposition I: *Philosophy must constitute itself as the theory of what we do and not as the theory of what is, because thought only says what it is by saying what it does: re-constructing immanence by replacing abstract units with concrete multiplicities, the IS of unification with the AND qua process (a multiplicity for each and every thing, a world of non-totalizable fragments communicating through external relations).*

*

The work on Bergson, undertaken right after the publication of *Empiricism and Subjectivity*, with the two articles published in 1956 ('Bergson, 1859–1941' and 'The Conception of Difference in Bergson'), systematized ten years later in *Bergsonism* (1966) – and not *Bergson*, like there was a *Nietzsche*, a *Spinoza*, a *Foucault*, a *Leibniz* . . . (and also a *Kant* to which we'll need to come back) – is concerned with thinking the question of Monism as the vitalist affirmation of Difference in the irreducible multiplicity of becoming. For being cannot equal itself without remainder to difference unless difference is recast as *differentiation*, that is, as process and creation, individuation *as* process (*élan vital*); unless – on the basis of a virtual which, without being actual, possesses as such an *intensive reality* (an abstract intensive quantity) endowed with a power of singularization through remarkable points – one attains the pure essence of a non-chronological Time. ('It is the passing present which defines the actual', implying already constituted individuals; but 'it is in the virtual that the past is conserved'.) Power-time [*Temps-puissance*] against State-of-affairs [*État-des-lieux*], *the distinction between virtual and actual corresponds to the most fundamental scission of Time*. Arranging a relation of immanence of the virtual to its actualization, that is, a sort of *crystallization* between the virtual and the actual where there is no longer any assignable limit between them, there surges up the crystal-image, the time crystal unearthed by Deleuze at the heart of cinematographic creation, in the image of the Lady of Shanghai . . .

Grafted onto a critique of the category of the possible which throws back upon itself a ready made and preformed real and, in the same throw, undertakes a critique of the sovereignty of the negative and of dialectical opposition as *false movement*, Bergsonist vitalism is invested in such a way as to permit the affirmation of the existence of a *differential ontological unconscious*, whose conical volume occludes any dualism between the sensible and the intelligible, matter and duration. 'Duration differs from matter because it is first and foremost what differs from itself, so that the matter from which it differs is still duration': matter is the lowest degree of difference (like distension in relation to contraction, or the actual with regard to the virtual).

There lies the whole Bergsonian dimension of the formula proposed by Deleuze – 'pluralism = monism' – which only acquires meaning when multiplicity is conceived as a genuine substantive, situated prior to the dialectical opposition of the one and the multiple, which has been replaced with the difference between two types of multiplicity: numerical, material and actual multiplicity, a distinct multiplicity implying space as one of the conditions that must also be explained on its basis (Riemann); and qualitative multiplicity, which implies duration *qua* virtual coexistence of the one and the multiple, *neither* one *nor* multiple, *a* multiplicity . . . Deleuze will never cease returning to the revolution introduced by Bergson in the second chapter of *Time and Free Will*, where the space/duration polarity is only set out for the sake of the preliminary and more profound theme of the two multiplicities, where it is a question of relating

92   *Appendix I*

pure duration to the idea of a pure heterogeneity. 'Differen*t*iated without being differen*c*iated', an internal difference which is 'differential in itself and differentiating in its effect': this complex, to be designated by the name of different/ciation imposes virtuality as the very object of the theory *into which praxis must install itself in order to promote an ever-nomadic subject*, 'made of individuations, but impersonal ones, or of singularities, but pre-individual ones'.[10]

That is how Deleuze could recognize himself in a certain structuralism (it is after all the principle behind his response to the question 'How Do We Recognize Structuralism?': by seeing structure as virtuality, as the multiplicity of virtual coexistences effectuating themselves at diverse rhythms in accordance with a multi-serial time of actualization . . .), before denouncing structuralism's incapacity to account for a reality proper to becoming in a later text from *A Thousand Plateaus*: 'Memories of a Bergsonian'.

For it was in the wake of his Bergsonian studies[11] that Deleuze could oppose to the sedentary character of numerical individuation the nomadic insistence of the virtual in the actual, the pure spatio-temporal dynamism designed to let us grasp the world in its ideal eventality and 'real experience in all its particularities' (heterogenesis). Whence a second proposition which sums up this experimental naturalism for which *philosophy merges with ontology* and *ontology merges with the univocity of Being* (according to the famous formulae of *The Logic of Sense*[12]):

Proposition II: *Philosophy is indissociable from a theory of intensive multiplicities insofar as intuition as method is an anti-dialectical*

---

[10] ['À quoi reconnaît-on le structuralisme?', in *L'île déserte et autres texts. Texts et entretiens 1953–1974*, ed. David Lapoujade (Paris: Minuit, 2002), p. 267; 'How Do We Recognize Structuralism?', trans. Melissa McMahon and Charles J. Stivale, *Desert Islands and Other Texts, 1953–1974*, ed. David Lapoujade (New York: Semiotext(e), 2004), p. 190.]

[11] Published in 1973 in the collection *L'Histoire de la philosophie* edited by François Châtelet (Paris: Marabout, 1979, new abridged edition), the article entitled 'How Do We Recognize Structuralism?' opens with the phrase 'We are in 1967' – that is, a year after the publication of *Bergsonism*. That explains in part *how* the virtualization of structuralism conditions *The Logic of Sense* (1969).

[12] [*The Logic of Sense*, p. 179.]

method of research and affirmation of difference in the play of the actual and the virtual.

*

The simultaneous discovery of Bergson and Nietzsche – Nietzsche or the Return of difference which would allow Deleuze to push further the exploration of the *practical element of difference qua ontological affirmation raised to its highest power* in the differential field of forces, sense and value. With *Nietzsche and Philosophy* (1962), once it is postulated that sense only appears in the relation between the thing and the force of which it is the *sign* (and every sign, in this sense, demands an *evaluation* itself caught up in the logic of forces: force is the affirmation of a point of view[13]); it is the being of difference as such, stripped of any form of interiority (of the soul, of essence or of the concept), which finds itself affirmed in the doctrine of the Eternal Return. By having invested will as the differential element of force, the Eternal Return frees itself from the curvature of the circle only so as to allow the return of what either affirms or is affirmed. An unexpected relay of pure Bergsonian memory, in the joy of becoming-active 'returning is the being of difference which excludes the whole of the negative' by including the entirety of the singular. Being as a living being, the return of difference as a form of vital experience, when 'selection no longer concerns the claim [*prétention*], but power [*puissance*]' (according to the definitive formula of 'Plato, the Greeks'[14] – the modesty of power, against the claim of the Rivals . . .). For if Nietzsche denounces like none before him all the mystifications that disfigure philosophy and divert thought from the affirmation of life (from the ascetic ideal to the moral ideal, from the moral ideal to the ideal

[13] This theme will be differently developed in *Proust and Signs* (1964, 1970 for the expanded edition). This question of the sign-sense has been masterfully expounded by François Zourabichvili in *Deleuze. Une philosophie de l'événement* (Paris: PUF, 1994), see the section entitled 'Rencontre, signe, affect'.

[14] [*Essays Critical and Clinical*, p. 137.]

of knowledge, with humanism as *the deepest and most superficial* of mystifications: the superior man, the veridical man, a prodigious chain of counterfeiters . . .), it is because he will have been the first to dare inscribe *upon a body the relation with the outside as a field of forces and intensities*: 'the body of the Earth, the body of the book, the body of Nietzsche suffering', returning in all the names of history ('Nomad Thought'[15]) – *that is to say* my own body insofar as it is not Flesh and no longer has a Self at its centre, Body without Organs . . .

Proposition III: *If the affirmation of the multiple is the speculative proposition and joy in the diverse the practical proposition, then we must affirm philosophy as this nomad thought that creates concepts as so many manners of being and modes of existence.*

*

With *Spinoza: Expressionism in Philosophy* (1968) and the many reprises Spinoza demanded (*Spinoza* [1970]; *Spinoza: Practical Philosophy* [1981]; 'On Spinoza' in *Dialogues* [1977] and *Negotiations* [1990]; 'Memories of a Spinozist' but also 'How to Make Oneself a Body without Organs' in *A Thousand Plateaus* [1980], since 'finally, isn't the *Ethics* the great book on the BwO?'; *What is Philosophy?* [1991], where Spinoza is bestowed the title of 'prince of philosophy', 'prince of immanence' . . .; 'Spinoza and the Three *Ethics*', which concludes *Essays Critical and Clinical* [1993]), we arrive at the celebration of 'the great Nietzsche-Spinoza identity' toward which 'everything tended'. This is because Spinoza deploys that same passage, reopened by Nietzsche's hammer blows, capable of linking Bergsonian ontology, Deleuze's Bergsonism, to an *ethics of expression as the constitutive activity of being*,[16] the establishment and construction of a common plane of immanence. 'For at the same time it is fully

[15] [In David B. Allison (ed.), *The New Nietzsche: Contemporary Styles of Interpretation* (Cambridge, MA: The MIT Press, 1985).]

[16] See Michael Hardt, *Gilles Deleuze: An Apprenticeship in Philosophy*, Chapter 3; together with my review in *Critique* 560–1 (1994), entitled 'Deleuze, philosophie pratique?'.

a plane of immanence, and yet it has to be constructed if one is to live in a Spinozist manner.'[17]

Taking Spinoza by the middle in this way ('us in the middle of Spinoza', as Deleuze says[18]), we immediately perceive that he embodies the extreme philosophical danger, the danger of absolute immanence and univocity, because he possesses the simplest formula, the formula that completes philosophy by *elevating* the non-philosophical: 'the immanence of expression in what expresses itself, and of the expressed in expression'.[19] Here the power of being returns in the *conatus* as the power of thinking, because the interior is only a selected exterior and the exterior a projected interior . . . Here the power of thinking is defined by the affects it is capable of producing in order to individuate the life that envelops it and to 'explicate' the desire which it is inseparable from as both potential and event. Whence the fact that philosophical concepts, following on from Spinozist 'common notions', are susceptible to a *biological evaluation relating back in the last instance to the body as model* and to the 'powers to affect and be affected that characterise each and every thing' on the Plane of Life. In the face of the whole of Nature a single abstract Animal, infinitely variable and transformable (affects are becomings), for all the assemblages effectuating it and for all the concepts expressing it.

Proposition IV: *As an Ethics of Thought-Being, an ethics of relations countering the doctrines of judgment with the powers of life, philosophy is an onto-ethology insofar as its concepts form so many possible worlds and events extracted from the movement of an infinite real-virtual.*

*

---

[17] ['Spinoza and Us', in *Spinoza: Practical Philosophy*, pp. 122–3.]

[18] [*Spinoza: Practical Philosophy*, p. 122.]

[19] It is hard to see how François Laruelle, in the name of a generalized (?) non-philosophy, can deduce from the 'mixture of immanence and the multiple' any kind of 'pure form of transcendence' . . . On the other hand, we can understand why this author lays claim to the Axioms of a non-Spinozist thought. See François Laruelle, 'Réponse à Deleuze' in *La Non-philosophie des contemporains*, ed. Non-philosophie, le Collectif (Paris: Kimé, 1995), pp. 49–78.

In light of the progressive establishment of this Frame, it is difficult at first to grasp the meaning of the work on Kant, with the
book from 1963 (*Kant's Critical Philosophy*) and its entirely
unexpected reprise in the 1986 article: 'On Four Poetic Formulae
that could Sum Up Kantian Philosophy' (reprinted in *Essays
Critical and Clinical*). When Deleuze spoke about this work, it
was to point out it was envisaged as 'a book on an enemy', with
the goal of showing 'how he functions, what are his gears' . . .
keeping in mind that *even Kant, when he condemns the transcendent use of the syntheses, is led to erect a plane of immanence, even
though he restricts himself to possible experience and does not
venture into real experimentation* (see *Negotiations*). The criti-
cism, developed in *Difference and Repetition* and taken up in *The
Logic of Sense*, amounts to showing that Kant does not do what
he says and does not say what he does, inasmuch as he limits
himself to tracing the transcendental from the features of the
empirical, thereby failing to produce a veritable genesis that
would move beyond the plan of representation – a plan that is
the condition of (possible) experience of an already individuated
real and that can only conceive of the diverse as imprisoned in
the *a priori* unity of the subject and object. But the 'net [is] so
slack that even the biggest fish slip through',[20] since these categories are both too general and too individual to account for the
sensible. Thus, it will be necessary to plunge into the matter of
sensibility so as to extract its transcendental character and *give
transcendental aesthetics a real status* – and no longer a merely
formal one, which is the case so long as sensations are referred
back to the *a priori* form of their representation – freeing the play
of singularities from a time subjected to the primacy of the categories of consciousness . . .[21] We re-encounter here the
Bergsonian chronology which borders on both sides *Kant's
Critical Philosophy*.

Notwithstanding that link, the critique of Kant does introduce a new dimension in the Deleuzian history of philosophy by

[20] [*Bergsonism*, p. 45, translation modified.]
[21] You will find in Jean-Clet Martin's fine book all the variations of Deleuzian
'demonstration'. See *Variations. La philosophie de Gilles Deleuze* (Paris: Payot,
1993).

deploying a function of *counter-effectuation* in which the problematic position of modernity comes to inscribe itself.

This takes place at a twofold level.

First of all, it is the book on Kant that bears the subtitle *The Doctrine of the Faculties* and that engages the *Critique of Judgment*, in order to show that only aesthetic common sense can serve as the object of a properly transcendental genesis, to the extent it manifests the existence of a free and undetermined accord between the faculties, and that this accord forms the 'living ground' presupposed by every determinate accord under a determinant and legislative faculty (understanding: logical common sense; reason: moral common sense). 'Consequently aesthetic common sense does not complete the two others; *it grounds them or makes them possible*',[22] by moving beyond the beautiful form, by attaching itself to the matter employed by nature to produce the beautiful, a fluid and crystalline matter that doubles the formal aesthetics of taste with a '*material* meta-aesthetics'. Kantian romanticism would thus be the bearer of a Copernican revolution entirely different from the one announcing the 'classical' submission of the nondescript object [*l'objet quelconque*] to the logical subject (of common sense), a revolution capable, in a relation of radical immanence, of investing the very being of the sensible as the stakes of a transcendental empiricism – in the guise of a *new transcendental aesthetics*. Put in yet another way, in a characteristically Deleuzian turn of phrase: 'determining judgment and reflective judgment are not like two species of the same genus. Reflective judgment manifests and liberates a depth which remained hidden in the other. But the other was also judgment only by virtue of this living depth.'[23]

With the article on the four poetic formulae 'that could sum up Kantian philosophy', Deleuze is no longer concerned with retrieving the constitutive lines of force of the textual elaboration of the transcendental method but, more radically, with subjecting Kantian thought to *the heterogenesis of its unthought* in order to carry it off towards an outside elsewhere explored in

---

[22] [*Kant's Critical Philosophy*, pp. 49–50.]
[23] [*Kant's Critical Philosophy*, p. 60.]

terms of *capitalism and schizophrenia* (according to the general title of *Anti-Oedipus* and *A Thousand Plateaus*).

Four great reversals can be defined on this basis:

1. The reversal of time in relation to the cardinal movements of the world, with the time *'out of joint'* which discovers itself as the pure order of time, as 'the time of the city and nothing else'.

2. The reversal of time in relation to the intensive movement of the soul,[24] with the discovery of the *thread of time* which never ceases to relate the I to the Self under the condition of a fundamental difference: 'I is another', or the paradox of inner sense, when 'the madness of the subject corresponds to the time out of joint'.

3. The reversal of the Law – elevated to its pure and empty uniqueness – in relation to the Good, which brings us the announcement of the Kafkian time of deferred judgement and infinite debt.

4. The establishment of an aesthetics of the beautiful and the sublime which proposes we undertake an exercise at the limits of the faculties, the derangement of all the senses, 'in order to form strange combinations as sources of time' . . .

When the history of philosophy becomes the thought experiment of a time placed under the sign of its elements of curvature, declination, inflection, creative bifurcation . . . where 'the before and after no longer point to anything but an order of superimpositions' and one is consequently led to consider, in terms of a modern image of thought, *the time of philosophy and the philosophy of time rather than the history of philosophy*.

Scholium 1: *From a philosophical point of view, the history of philosophy is only worth our while if it begins to introduce some philosophical time into the time of history. It is a matter of becomings that wrest history away from itself, turning it into a universal history of a principle of contingent reason, so that one will be able to conceive of it as the milieu in which is negotiated the necessary*

---

[24] [In his preface to Alliez's 1991 *Capital Times*, Deleuze himself says 'we need a mutation of thought in order to define time as the cipher of the intensive movement of the soul'. Now reprinted as 'Préface: Les allures du temps' in *Deux régimes de fous et autres textes*, p. 349.]

intersection of philosophy with history as a whole, but also with the sciences and arts.

*

By deploying the World-Thought of a Leibnizian transcendental philosophy 'which bears on the event rather than the phenomenon, replaces Kantian conditioning with a double operation of transcendental actualisation and realisation (animism and materialism)',[25] Deleuze's last book on a philosopher, *The Fold: Leibniz and the Baroque* (1988), furnishes us with that philosophy's impeccable *manner*. But how can we think the event associated with the name of Leibniz – to wit, that of an evental theory of the singular guaranteeing the interiority of the concept and the individual, assuming the concept as a metaphysical being that partakes in a world all of whose relations are internal (monadology): with regard to Deleuze's itinerary in the history of philosophy, which began with empiricism, something here closes the loop, a loop or a *fold* that will make of his next book (with Guattari) a narration in the direct style of the world-being of philosophy *itself* (a nomadology)? How can we enter the Leibnizian universe without repeating the material gesture that freed the baroque machines (the fold that goes all the way to the infinite), without restoring the operational act that was able to define their properly metaphysical point of inherence and which constitutes the contribution of Leibnizianism to philosophy (the paradigm of the fold as the 'organicist' method of the elevation of thought to the infinite of the labyrinthine play of the world)? How can we do this without reliving 'the marriage of the concept and singularity' and re-encountering a whole Bergsonism present among Leibniz's themes in the formula *Omnis in unum*? It is thus in a single movement that one will be able to *see* 'how much Leibniz is part of this [baroque] world, for which he provides the philosophy it lacks,'[26] and to *fold* the Leibnizian text in order to envelop

[25] [*The Fold*, p. 163/120.]
[26] [*The Fold*, p. 173/126.]

it in our chaotic world, constituted by divergent series that no
longer resolve themselves into accords (chaosmos: the divergent
game). To compose a new Baroque . . .
  Fold by fold, a neo-Leibnizianism emerges thereby as a way of
addressing the modern image of thought in its processes of com-
possibilization of the most radical heterogeneities.[27] *In other
words, the affirmation of a virtual Leibnizianism implying real
Leibnizianism as its restricted version* – restricted to the last
attempt to reconstitute a classical reason . . . 'in a new type of
story in which [. . .] description takes the place of the object, the
concept becomes narrative and the subject a point of view, a
subject of enunciation'.
  We can now fully understand Alain Badiou's observation,
according to which this definition of the baroque superbly fits
the Deleuzian *manner*, in its power of narration into which every
Subject resolves itself, for the benefit of the Signature of the
world Leibniz-Bergson-Deleuze.[28]

Scholium 2: *There can be a philosophical history of philosophy
only through the elaboration of virtual philosophies that dramatize
a play of concepts as the expression of a play of the world. Such a
history does not have one particular philosophy or another as its
object, but rather takes it as a point of view, as a pure effectiveness
comprehending its real, (trans-)historical, effectuation, like the
initial inflection and original folding of an ideality in itself inseparable from an infinite variation. That is the ground of Deleuzian
perspectivism: the Fold as the operator of the Multiple, singularizing from the vantage point of this immanence the individuation of
thought in each of the world's folds.*

* * *

Like a spider continually reweaving his web, Deleuze extracts
and selects from each of 'his' philosophers a virtual universe of

[27] [*The Fold*, p. 174/127. *Pli selon pli* (*Fold by Fold*) is the title of a composition by Pierre Boulez devoted to the work of Stéphane Mallarmé.]
[28] Alain Badiou, 'Gilles Deleuze, *The Fold: Leibniz and the Baroque*', p. 57.

concepts which he folds onto a real world of forces, such that these philosophers will constitute the only 'subjects' of his philosophy (the altruistic principle of every generous reading, since one is never served better than by one's others), destined to be invested as so many heteronyms, so many intercessors, so many conceptual personae resonating with one another in a multiplied theatre in which the masked ball *carries the power of the false to a degree which no longer effectuates itself in form* (the counterfeit) *but in transformation*: 'The Mystery of Ariadne according to Nietzsche,' here lies Deleuze's profound Nietzscheanism in his use of proper names, upon which he imprints a veritable *becoming-concept*.[29] Deleuzian heterogenesis and transmutation are thus given as (better: *they give us*) ontogenesis as a world-philosophy investing the plane of immanence or univocity as the radical field of experience of an over-physics freed of every Form; the critique of all essential, substantial or functional forms, the critique of all forms of transcendence (including in its latest, phenomenological, figure, when the time comes to think transcendence within immanence[30]), through which the entirety of the history of philosophy will have 'passed' *once it is put in continuous variation.* Whence the unique character of the Deleuzian affirmation of philosophy as system. In effect, 'the system must not only be in perpetual heterogeneity, it must be a *heterogenesis*, which is something I think *has never been attempted*' (my emphasis).[31]

What has never been attempted is this systematic virtualization of the history of philosophy as the mode of actualization of *a* new philosophy, of a *virtual* philosophy whose infinitely

---

[29] Once again I intersect here the analysis of Nancy, who remarks that Deleuzian philosophy impresses *in parallel* on the 'becoming-concept' of proper names a 'becoming-proper-name' to certain concepts (we could mention the plateau or the rhizome, the refrain or the fold . . .).

[30] See above, chapter III of *The Signature of the World*, 'Onto-Ethologics'; and especially my *De l'impossibilité de la phenomenology. Sur la philosophie française contemporaine* (Paris: Vrin, 1995), Chapter II – 'Positions de la philosophie'.

[31] Extracted from Deleuze's 'Letter-Preface' to Jean-Clet Martin's book (now reprinted in *Deux régimes de fous et autres textes*, pp. 338–340), this affirmation takes on a rather unique status in the Deleuzian corpus.

variable effectuation does not cease to *make folds* (folds by folds), thus setting Deleuze apart from the author-function *and* from the false enunciation of the commentator – to the benefit of an infinitely more 'baroque' and Borgésian figure: mannerism.

(These are the two reproaches which have always been made against Deleuze: he is not an author because he comments, but neither is he a commentator because what he writes is always 'Deleuzian'.)

To grasp Deleuzian philosophy as this virtual phenomenology of the concept whose creative and 'onturgic' power cannot project itself into the Open of thought without by the same token returning as the manner and matter of Being, the deployment on the plane of Nature or composition of an ontology of experience that does not trace the transcendental from the empirical, as Kant did: '[the transcendental] must therefore be explored on its own, that is "experimented" (but through a very particular type of experience)' . . . The mannerism of a continuous creation, both territorial and deterritorialized, becoming infinite in between the interior forces of the Earth and the exterior forces of Chaos, in order to make flee the Thousand Plateaus of a 'molecular pantheist Cosmos' – on an obscure background of enveloping animality (to borrow Alain Badiou's magnificent expression). An opera-machine for 'an immense abstract Machine, which is nevertheless real and individual', to which Deleuze, in the last book written with Félix Guattari (*What is Philosophy?*; but see already *Rhizome* [1976]), gives the sober and luminous name of Brain-Thought.

When the world discovers itself as brain, once 'expression and production open themselves up to the materiality of the modern'[32] and the man/machine relation becomes expressive/productive of a becoming that no longer possesses a subject distinct from itself, from an outside and an inside: 'collective, temporal and nervous rhizome' (*A Thousand Plateaus*); a becoming carrying along with it thought as the *auto-objectivation* of Nature by differential relations, 'now that any distinction between nature and artifice is

[32] Antonio Negri, 'On Gilles Deleuze & Félix Guattari, *A Thousand Plateaus*', *Graduate Faculty Philosophy Journal* 18(2), 1995.

becoming blurred'.[33] Brain-World: independently of any content, far from every object, this philosophy is that of the Implication of the Modern in the Idea of an Inside of the pure Outside, in the complicated sense of the Leibnizian genitive which already rendered all perception hallucinatory (because perception has no object).

Thus Deleuze's question will always have been that of a material and virtual-actual image of Thought-Being, of the rhizome and of immanence, with the superior ethology it calls for in order to follow the unknown furrows traced in the world-brain by every free creation of concepts: new connections, new passages, new synapses for new compositions which make the singular into a concept . . .

An entire pragmatics of the concept as real being, absolute volume, self-bearing surface, crystallization and coalescence, fold of the brain onto itself, *micro-brain* . . . a whole 'machinics' of thought will thus be mobilized in order to *make the multiple* (for 'we need a method to do it effectively'), to *take the virtual as subject* ('the actualisation of the virtual is the singularity') and finally respond to the question 'what is philosophy?' ('philosophy is the theory of multiplicities') – when old age comes, and so does the hour to speak concretely, at the singular point in which concept and creation relate to one another in the great identity EXPRESSIONISM = CONSTRUCTIVISM.

Gilles Deleuze
or
the OFF-SUBJECT of philosophy
and
the OPEN PLANE of thought

a virtual philosophy
for all and some.[34]

Translated by Alberto Toscano

---

[33] [*Negotiations*, p. 212/155.]

[34] ['Off-subject' here translates *hors-sujet*, literally 'off the subject', but could also be rendered as 'out-subject'.]

Appendix II On the Philosophy of Gilles Deleuze: An Introduction to Matter*

An *ontology of the virtual* – or a *materialism of the virtual* – that is how I think we could define the Deleuzian image of thought, as it forces itself upon us at all the levels of his philosophy.

Historically, or historiographically, that is what is at stake, in my view, in the Bergsonian studies undertaken right after the publication of *Empiricism and Subjectivity*, with the two articles published in 1956 ('Bergson, 1859–1941' and above all 'The Conception of Difference in Bergson'[1]), systematized ten years later in *Bergsonism* (1966) – and not simply *Bergson*, like there are, among Deleuze's publications, a *Nietzsche*, a *Kant*, a *Spinoza*, a *Foucault* . . . These studies will provide the backbone for the core chapters of *Difference and Repetition* (1968), a book that should be conceived as the matrix of Deleuzism; the titles of these chapters are: 'The Image of Thought', 'The Ideal Synthesis of Difference', 'The Asymmetrical Synthesis of the Sensible'. The role of these early studies can be felt all the way to the last, posthumously published, text, which takes up again the question of philosophy as a 'theory of multiplicities', under the title 'The Actual and the Virtual'.[2] So

* [Originally published in French as 'Sur la philosophie de Gilles Deleuze: une entrée en matière', in *Gilles Deleuze: Immanence et vie*, ed. Éric Alliez at al., *Rue Descartes* 20 (Paris: PUF, 1998).]

[1] See 'Bergson, 1859–1941', trans. Christopher Busch, and 'Bergson's Conception of Difference', trans. Michael Taormina, in *Desert Islands and Other Texts, 1953–1974*, pp. 28–42/22–31 and 43–72/32–51.

[2] This text was added to the second edition of *Dialogues*, with Claire Parnet (Paris: Flammarion, 1996) and can now be found in Eliot Ross Albert's English translation in *Dialogues II* (London: Continuum, 2002).

many signs, so many indices that make us think that invoking –
under the rubric of a chaosmic virtual – a *bergsonism of Deleuze*
could lead us to grasp *in flagrante* the heterogenesis *in actu* of this
thought, at the level of both system (since Deleuze, hardly a post-
modernist in this regard, equates philosophy with system) and
method (in Bergson-Deleuze intuition becomes a method – no less
rigorous and demanding than the geometrical method).

But what precisely is an *ontology of the virtual?* If every ontology turns around the question of being it means we need to risk
problematizing being qua virtual.

I don't think I'm forcing the texts by forwarding the hypothesis
that this problematization is set out on the basis of a reversal of
the 'ontological argument' formulated by the philosophical tradition, from Saint Anselm to Hegel passing through Descartes,
as *a priori* proof of the existence of God. This quasi-genetic
foundation of idealism allowed one to conclude, in the abstract
identity of the concept, from the possibility of the existence of
God to the affirmation of his reality, based on the fact that the
reality of his existence is part of the very definition of the
concept of God . . . This tradition is that of onto-theology in its
modern configuration. But remove the name of God from this
demonstration and you will witness the emergence of the purest
form of the logical ideal (or the 'theorematic' ideal, according to
Deleuze's expression) of mathematical representation, when that
representation claims to guarantee *a priori* the correlation
between thought and the most abstract being, emptied of any
materiality by its absolute depotentialization . . .[3]

It is this conception which is opposed by the philosophical
notion of the virtual. In its simplest formulation, of a strictly
Bergsonian type: The virtual is not actual but as such possesses
an ontological reality that contests and exceeds any logic of the
possible.

The possible is effectively the logical category that posits, from
the point of view of the identity of the concept, that there is no

---

[3] Whilst 'the most closed system still has a thread that rises toward the virtual,
and down which the spider descends'. See *What is Philosophy?*, p. 116/122.

difference between the possible and the real, *since we have already given ourselves everything* [*puisqu'on s'est déjà tout donné*], preformed 'in the pseudo-actuality of the possible'.[4] It is this classical figure of the argument, erroneously dubbed 'ontological', which grounds the philosophy of representation and the system of recognition: it posits that existence is the same thing as the concept but lies outside it, in a milieu indifferent to any sensorial dynamism, a milieu of the assimilation of time to a space homogenized in its totality (*All* is given [*Tout est donnée*]). In short, the category of the possible homogenizes being as well as thought because the *subject* of representation determines the *object* as *really* conforming to the concept understood as essence. Therefore, this essence *will only ever define the conditions of possible experience, which will resemble real experience only because the condition refers back to the conditioned, whose actual image it traces in its own likeness.* In short, as Deleuze explains following Bergson, the possible is always constructed after the fact, since it has been 'arbitrarily extracted from the real, like a sterile double'.[5] This explains why, according to Deleuze's diagnosis, both Kant and Husserl had to abandon the genesis of the given and the constitution of the *real* transcendental field, since the given is always already given as an object to a subject, in accordance with the principle of natural perception (a naturally phenomeno-logical perception). Working with this mimetic vision of beings [*l'étant*] they remained prisoner to the logic of the alternative *all or nothing*, which has always associated cosmology and psychology to theology by prohibiting *the leap into ontology*: '*either* an undifferentiated ground, a groundlessness, formless nonbeing or an abyss without differences and without properties *or* a supremely individuated Being and an intensely personalised Form. Without this Being or this Form, you will have nothing but chaos . . .'[6]

Dialectics cannot evade that alternative, since the forms of the

---

[4] [*Bergsonism*, p. 98.]

[5] Bachelard's famous formula according to which 'the real is one of the forms of the possible' is thus reversed: it is the possible which is now nothing more than a form of the real . . .

[6] [*The Logic of Sense*, p. 129/106. Translation modified.]

negative can account for actual terms and real relations between states of affairs only *insofar as they have been cut off from the virtuality they actualize and the movement of their actualization,* which does *not* resemble the virtuality that is incorporated and materialized by this movement. This is an extremely important point that governs the entirety of Deleuzian philosophy, to the extent that the latter opens itself up to Bergson's injunction as a *philosophy of difference*: far from realizing itself through resemblance, the virtual actualizes itself by differentiating itself, such that in the play of a difference without negation, actualization is the creation of the new, it is individuation. It is a continuous creation of differences, or a production of divergences, in accordance with a model which is no longer mathematical but rather biological, that is, *ontobiological* and *vitalist*, insofar as it implies an intense, pre-individual field of singularities, tantamount to a genuine *introduction to (the) matter*[7] of philosophy in its *pre-immanence*. In other words, we are dealing with the opposite of an abstract universal (the virtual is neither a 'category' nor a 'principle'). This model is that of an *élan vital* or a 'creative evolution' (Bergson), an 'individuation' and an 'ontogenesis' (Simondon), or a 'heterogenesis' (Deleuze), which makes the *ontological difference* – a theme that here acquires a rigorously non-Heideggerian meaning – pass between the virtual-material from which one begins and the actual-individuals to which one arrives. This takes place in a manner akin to that in which an intensity explicates itself, develops itself in an extensity [*extension*] which is related to the extension [*étendue*] that tends to annul its constituent differences, even if the latter constitute the very being of the sensible. It is indeed intensity, through the essential process of intensive quantities (in other words, 'dynamic quanta', *forces* understood as 'relations between relations', according to Bergson's formulation – i.e. *multiplicities*) which determines the actualization of differential relations into the qualities and extensions it creates through individuation. Moreover, if indeed there exists an ontological difference in

---

[7] [*Une entrée en matière*, literally 'an entrance into matter', is usually used to signify an introduction to a topic, the broaching of a subject.]

Deleuze, it deploys itself on a plane defined by the originally Bergsonian duality between geometric space and open duration, the extended and the intensive, between what I will call *material* [*matériel*] and *materiel* [*matérial*]; by the distinction between two types of multiplicity, metric and non-metric, homogeneous and heterogeneous: quantitative multiplicities of exteriority and internal qualitative multiplicities. Thus we have, on the one hand, continuous multiplicities of a virtual order, belonging essentially to duration, which cannot divide without thereby changing in kind each and every time, since they are not constituted by a set of distinct terms but rather by elements 'in fusion' that welcome the new in its becoming insofar as it is necessarily heterogeneous to what precedes it . . . in other words, we are dealing with a multiplicity of an ordinal type, which amounts to a veritable transcendental principle adequate to becoming; on the other hand, we have actual discontinuous multiplicities, empirically represented by homogeneous space in accordance with the cardinal regime of *partes extra partes*.[8] And, operating a kind of to and fro movement between the two multiplicities – spatial and temporal, essentially biological (difference in kind) or essentially mechanical (difference in degree) – is *matter*, sometimes still enveloped in the *materiel* plane of immanence of qualitative multiplicity, sometimes already developed, organized, *materialized, metricized* [*métrisée*] in the system of reference of homogeneous magnitudes and geometric or organic forms. Having grasped this 'non-coincidence', which is the bearer of two absolutely antagonistic images of materialism, it suffices to invoke the reprise in *A Thousand Plateaus* of the theme of the Body without Organs (a 'body all the more alive and teeming once it has blown apart the organism and its organization . . .') on the basis of the distinction between Molar and

---

[8] Following a remark by Frederic Worms, we will note that 'the parts of time are only conserved in a whole by ceasing to be parts, which in effect they have never *been*; we can only think their conservation by ceasing to *think* them as parts, that is basically as instants. More precisely still, the parts of time are only *virtual* parts, which actualization by our reflection will change in kind, since such an actualization presupposes a juxtaposition in space which extracts them from their immanent succession.' See Frederic Worms, 'La conception bergsonienne du temps', *Philosophie* 54 (1997), p. 79.

Molecular,[9] Smooth and Striated, in order to see that it is indeed
the whole of Deleuze's Bergsonism which is mobilized in the
affirmation that 'philosophy [*la* philosophie] is the theory of
multiplicities', according to the formula that opens the last,
posthumous text – a formula, allow me to note, which is systematically ignored by Badiou in *his* Deleuze.[10] In these incredibly
dense pages, whose title and content could not be any more
Bergsonian – 'The Actual and the Virtual' – we encounter one
last time the statement of the essential tenet of Deleuze's philosophy, to wit that we will only attain the plane of immanence by
conferring upon the virtual a full *materiality* upon which
depends its actualization *qua* different/ciation into an actuality
determined in and by 'functions'. Thus 'the actual is the complement or the product, the object of actualization, but the only
subject of the latter is the virtual'. And, as its '*de jure* subject,
insofar as it is in the making, [. . .] life, as the bearer of singularities'.[11]

That the name of Being be Life as immanent power, the living
production of its modes, and that ontology become indissociable
from the constitution of a bio-politics; that philosophy be developed as a 'theory of multiplicities' and that, by the same token,
it constitute a *politics of being*, extending itself into an analysis
of power that will double the history of its forms of expression

---

[9] See *A Thousand Plateaus*, p. 264/217: 'the molar and the molecular are distinguished not only by size, scale or dimension but by the nature of the system
of reference envisioned' [translation modified].

[10] We will limit ourselves here to recalling that Deleuze's entire philosophy is
developed *within* the rigorous articulation between 'philosophy of the univocity
of being' and 'theory of multiplicities'. That is, in an *ontology of the virtual*. This
is sufficient to state what Deleuzian thought is not: a metaphysics of the One
doomed to affirm the 'fictive character of the multiple'. Which is precisely what
Badiou practices, despite, or rather because of, his claim to a 'Platonism of the
multiple', at least in his exercises in textual commentary: in which it is always
necessary to bring the different back to the identical, multiplicity to the multiple and the multiple to the one, the singular to the non-contradictory, the concrete to the universality of a case, and so on. See Badiou's *Deleuze: The Clamor
of Being*, trans. Louise Burchill (Minneapolis: Minnesota University Press,
2000), and the Badiou/Deleuze dossier in *Futur Antérieur* 43 (1997–8), with articles by Arnaud Villani and José Gil, as well as the continuation of the debate in
Multitudes 1 (2000).

[11] *Foucault*, p. 97 [my translation].

with a becoming of the forces conditioning them (according to the distinction between abstract machine and concrete assemblages); that Being be said of becomings that 'fall back into history but do not come from it', and that philosophical time consequently must be thought as a 'grandiose time of co-existence', as 'an infinite becoming of philosophy that crosscuts its history without being confused with it'[12] – all these theses, which I have termed *onto-ethological* (see chapter III), must be immediately linked back [*mises à l'actif de*] to an *ontology of the virtual*, insofar as each of them manifests that the virtual is *not* a 'category' but the very source of a *(hetero-)genetic materialism* which invests 'zero intensity as a principle of production'[13]; a materialism which we could also call a *transcendental materialism* insofar as it is rigorously non-'generic', grafted onto the individuating becomings of being as singular arrangements of matter = energy *qua* auto-objective synthesis of heterogeneities, at a remove from any hylomorphic schema which would presuppose a homogenized matter, a matter prepared for an organizing form.

(To think, as Deleuze will say in his *Foucault*, is to attain the non-stratified by freeing life wherever it's imprisoned . . .)

Inasmuch as it is prior to the scission of time into two dissymmetrical jets – corresponding to the actual image of the passing present leaping toward the future and the virtual image of the past which is conserved *in itself* – everything Bergson said about *pure duration* comes down to the following: pure duration is what differs from itself in coexistence with itself through a non-chronological time, since what differs from itself is *immediately* a coexistence of the past with the present, the *contemporaneous* unity of being with becoming, substance with subject, in the *élan vital* which raises up difference to the absolute of a potential or a virtual, and forces thought *to begin with the materiality of difference* insofar as this materiality designates *the new in the making*. A *permanent individuation* by means of the first

---

[12] *What is Philosophy?*, pp. 92, 58/96, 59.
[13] [*A Thousand Plateaus*, p. 164.]

'transductiveness',[14] that of time implicating in its Open the
virtual dimension composed by the *concrete* totality of the past.

That is what Bergson evoked with a word which has lent itself
to so many misunderstandings (and was later taken up by
Simondon[15]): *intuition*. For intuition, inasmuch as it is occupied
with determining the conditions of real experience – and not the
generic conditions of an experience that is only possible for the
representation which projects behind difference something
endowed with resemblance – by seeking duration in things, by
plunging into a dimension prior to the subject and object distinction, in the pure form of time as the individuating becoming of
Being, must begin with the vital difference *that generates its own
intuitive movement*. This is an intuition *of* duration, according to
a genitive that is both objective and subjective; intuition is
thereby recognized as the *jouissance of difference*, in the movement that allows one to attain the virtual as a *pure concept of
difference*. Whence an eminently problematic image of thought
that knows how to render itself adequate to the univocal nature
of being as difference – 'being is the difference itself of the
thing'[16] – by affirming the ontobiological principle of the intellectual and *materiel* value of problems. After all, to differentiate
is to problematize, to *materialize* by engaging the virtual as the
problematic instance for which the actual proposes solutions.

To paraphrase Bergson, this *intuitive* and *problematic* method
will involve the reality of philosophy as an *experience* by manifesting the bad will required to 'chase away ready-made concepts'
– the concepts of representation – in order to pose problems
afresh, to match the articulations of the real and follow its ten-

[14] [The reference to *la première transductivité* is to Gilbert Simondon *L'individu
et sa genèse physico-biologique* (Grenoble: J. Millon, 1995 [1965]), p. 161.]

[15] See the Introduction to Gilbert Simondon, *L'individu et sa genèse physico-
biologique*: 'Transduction is therefore not only a mental process [*démarche de l'e-
sprit*]: it is also intuition, since it is that by which a structure appears in a
problematic domain as carrying the resolution of the problems posed therein.'
The principle of this operation of propagation which Simondon calls 'transduction' is defined as follows: 'each constituted region of the structure serves the
following regione as a principle of constitution' . . . It's fair to say that Simondon
offers us here something like a 'structural' reading of Bergson's *Creative
Evolution*.

[16] 'Bergson, 1859–1941', p. 32/25.

dencies rather than let oneself be guided by the conservative logic of common sense, which limits itself to choosing between solutions sedimented in language. This would explain why 'conversation resembles conservation', keeping in mind that Bergson – like Deleuze . . . – holds in low esteem the *homo loquax* 'whose thought, when he thinks, is a mere reflection on his speech', who bases his communication on a knowledge his interlocutors already possess; and that for a philosophy emancipated from the natural dialectic of words and things cut out by the understanding from the continuity of matter and life, to pose the problem is instead to *invent* and not only to dis-cover; it is to *create*, in the same movement, both the problem and its solution.[17] 'And I call a *philosopher* someone who creates the solution, which is then necessarily unique, of the problem that he has newly posed', with 'the new sense which words assume in the new conception of the problem'.[18] Without this overturning of common sense and this rupture with the *doxa* that entertains the logical ideal of recognition; without a *general theory of the problem* that no longer configures thought on the basis of 'solid' propositions supposed as pre-existent, but rather poses the problem as this ideal genetic and *extra-propositional* element of the production of the true; without this affirmation of the problematic as the differential intensity of Ideas themselves in their pre-immanence, a problematic irreducible to any kind of Analytic as well as to any kind of Dialectic, since it introduces duration and matter in thought, by reconciling truth and creation not only at the level of concepts but as this intensive state of the world constituted by the material reality of the virtual . . . – well, lacking this *speculative materialism* which is thus led to investing the opposition between the intuition of the 'in the making' and the analysis of the 'ready made' and, moreover, without the general reversal whereby 'being is said of becoming, identity of that which is different, the

---

[17] Henri Bergson, *La pensée et le mouvant*, translated as *An Introduction to Metaphysics: The Creative Mind* (Totowa, NJ: Littlefield, Adams & Co., 1975), 'Introduction (Part II): Stating the Problems'.

[18] Henri Bergson, 'Letter to Floris Delattre' [December 24, 1935], trans. Melissa McMahon, in *Key Writings*, ed. Keith Ansell Pearson and John Mullarkey (London: Continuum, 2002), pp. 370, 371.

one of the multiple, etc.', 'the famous Copernican revolution amounts to nothing'.[19]

That is the meaning of Bergsonism for Deleuze, a meaning he sums up at a very early date in a definitive formula: 'Life is the process of difference'[20] – and whose trace can be found as late as the following confession: 'Everything I've written has been vitalist, at least so I hope . . .'[21] It is effectively in this essential relationship with life that difference is differen*c*iation *qua* movement of a virtuality actualizing itself according to its own movement of internal difference (differen*t*iation). That is why there will be no rupture with regard to the thesis of the univocity of being to which Deleuze assimilates philosophy *qua* ontology, to the extent that what differentiates itself is first and foremost what differs from itself, to wit the virtual, a virtual which must indeed in its own fashion be real, materiel/material, in order to retain an objective, ontological consistency and be able to differentiate itself in the process of the production of the actual by virtue of its sub-representational efficacy (*virtus*, *in virtu*) . . . And doubtless, as Deleuze explains, 'the virtual is, in itself, the mode of the non-active, since it only acts in differentiating itself, in ceasing to be in itself, all the while keeping something of its origin. But it is in this very respect that it is the mode of *what is*'.[22] This is an absolute ante-predicative donation; under the univocal condition of time as 'the whole of relations,'[23] it is the *inside of the outside in its powerful nonorganic life*. In other words, quite precisely, the very *matterness* [*matièreté*] of being.

Here we find ourselves in a position that is in line with the one voiced in Nietzsche's famous phrase: 'To stamp upon becoming the character of being – this is the highest will to power'; and very close to the *sense* of the Bergson-Nietzsche intersection discovered by Deleuze via Simondon.

[19] *Difference and Repetition*, pp. 59, 210/40, 162.

[20] 'Bergson's Conception of Difference', p. 54/50.

[21] *Pourparlers* (Paris: Minuit, 1990), p. 196.

[22] 'Bergson's Conception of Difference', p. 62/55.

[23] Gilles Deleuze, *Cinéma 1. L'Image-mouvement* (Paris: Minuit, 1983); *Cinema 1: The Movement-Image*, trans. Hugh Tomlinson and Barbara Habberjam (London: Athlone Press, 1986), p. 21/10.

It is as a Nietzschean that Deleuze often returns to the first chapter of *Matter and Memory*, this book freed from psychology by the theme of the *attention to life*: short-circuiting the distinction between subject and object with his theory of 'matter-images',[24] Bergson attains the plane of immanence as pure experience, as the pure immanence of life to itself, displacing the opposition of life and matter in the direction of a 'continuity of durations' with – between matter and mind – all the possible intensities of a pure memory identical to the totality of the past, 'the past in general' existing in itself in the mode of a *virtual coexistence* ('the past is pure ontology'[25]); equality without remainder of being and life, implying the *de jure* coextension of consciousness and life, which thereby verifies its independence vis-à-vis the Self [*Moi*] in the identity of memory with duration itself. As Deleuze concludes: 'Subjectivity is never ours, it is time, that is [. . .] the virtual [. . .] and it is we who are internal to time, not the other way round.'[26] Because, as Bergson writes in *Matter and Memory*, 'it is the brain which is a part of the material world, and not the material world which is a part of the brain'.

It is as if Deleuze generalized, to cover the entirety of modern philosophy, Kantian and Hegelian, dialectical and phenomenological, the critique addressed by Bergson to Einstein: *that it confuses the actual and the virtual, having flattened the mathematical logic of cases of solution onto the ontological problematic of the question of matter and time.* In other words, it is to the extent that Deleuzian thought has the virtual as its sole subject that one will equally be able to call it a philosophy of becoming, of difference, of immanence or of the event – since it is the virtual that allows us, from the point of view of a truly transcendental materialism, to state each of these notions by itself and alongside the others.

It would not be difficult to show that the very constitution of

---

[24] Henri Bergson, *Matter and Memory*, Preface to the seventh edition: 'Matter, in our view, is an aggregate of "images" [. . .] but a self-existing image', trans. Nancy Margaret Paul and W. Scott Palmer (New York: Zone Books, 1991), pp. 9–10.
[25] [*Bergsonism*, p. 51/56.]
[26] Deleuze, *Cinema 2: The Time-Image*, pp. 110–1/82–3.

Deleuzian philosophy, in his monographs on Hume, Nietzsche, Spinoza, Leibniz, and so on, springs from a *systematic rematerialization* and *virtualization* of the history of philosophy[27] as the mode of actualization of *a* new philosophy, of a *virtual-materiel* philosophy whose infinitely variable effectuation does not cease producing new folds that implicate and complicate the 'infinite becoming of philosophy' *qua* theoretical practice of an immanence become absolute. It is thus – according to a formulation of Gilbert Simondon that carries Nietzsche and Deleuze in its phrasing – philosophy as the 'production of genetic essences', which always aims, via the concept, at something of the order of the *event*.

Whence the fact that the Deleuzian history of philosophy experiences the virtual-actual image of thought – a non-dogmatic, non-(re)cognitivist image, associating the concept to the point of emergence of the percept and the affect – by investing 'Bergsonism' as the intensive source of an ontology that will have lost, in one fell swoop, those phenomenological, dialectical and linguistic characteristics that encumber modern philosophy.

A non-idealist and non-humanist philosophy, a biophilosophy irreducible to every axiomatic capture – or, a *finally contemporary* materialist philosophy?[28]

Translated by Alberto Toscano

[27] For Deleuze, it is effectively always a question of *rematerializing* the history of philosophy by extracting the *gesture* of the philosopher (the Leibnizian fold, the Bergsonian bifurcation, etc.). To put it otherwise: once a philosophical corpus is given in its demonstrative formality, one will seek to engage the 'meta-aesthetics' which has never stopped generating it (in the mode of a continuous creation). Whence the acute attention lavished by Deleuze on the question of the *rhythms* and *speeds* of thought (his reading of Spinoza is exemplary in this regard). Deleuze never hid the Nietzschean inspiration that lay behind this 'method'.

[28] For some stimulating insights in this direction, based on a particularly interesting reading of *A Thousand Plateaus*, see Manuel DeLanda, 'Immanence and Transcendence in the Genesis of Form', in *A Deleuzian Century?*, ed. Ian Buchanan, *The South Atlantic Quarterly* 96/3 (1997).

Index